"I Am" Faithful

The Faithfulness of God

Dr. Jerry A. Grillo, Jr

Copyright
First Edition 2002
Jerry A. Grillo, Jr.
God's Unwavering Faithfulness
P.O. Box 3707
Hickory, NC. 28603

Second Edition 2014
FZM Publishing
"I Am" Faithful
P.O. Box 3707
Hickory, NC 28603

ISBN 978-0692313343

Printed in the United States of America.

Table of Content

INTRODUCTION

I guarantee that you haven't stumbled onto this book accidently. If you have lived your life like me you can testify that you haven't always been faithful. You haven't always been faithful to God, faithful in life, faithful in relationships, faithful with your money, faithful to your intentions, thoughts or yourself. I can say for a fact that God has always been faithful.

One of the most valuable thoughts of proving God's faithfulness is that no matter what you have lost because of rebellion or ignorance, God has promised to restore it. Restoration is the greatest proof of the faithfulness of God. Think about it. God gives us favor every day. We walk in common favor every morning when we wake up. Just getting out of bed is the proof of God's faithfulness to us. We are allowed to experience special favor every day. God has given us redemptive favor. There is not a moment in any day that we are not experiencing the faithfulness of God.

Another powerful proof of God's unwavering faithfulness is that He made provision to redeem us from our wrong decisions through Jesus. We can confess our sins and Jesus is faithful and just to forgive us of those sins. Salvation is a powerful gift.

Another powerful proof of God's faithfulness is that you can trust Him at His word. Numbers 23:19 is one of the greatest passages in the Bible. This passage expresses all we need to know about God. ***"God is not a man, that He should lie, if He said it, it will come to pass…"*** God is not a man. That's the most powerful part of this verse. God is God. God thinks like God, not like man. God moves like God, not like man. God wills what He wills, does what He wills and loves what He wills. God is God! The greatest mistake you can ever make is to try to make God human. He is not a human.

He is not a created being. He is the Creator! God's limit has no boundaries. This blows my mind. It boggles my understanding. Man has limits; God has none!

COVENANT IS GOD'S DOING

Covenant is a word that isn't used in today's language. We use words like contracts, agreements, and deals. God used the word "covenant." A handshake was legally binding at one time in history. However, as man began to walk further away from integrity...written contracts, documentation and notarization were required. Today it seems that you can't trust anyone to live up to what they have agreed to do. Many are quick to agree but few have the integrity to follow through.

INTEGRITY IS NEEDED

Integrity is lacking in our society. I had a friend tell me one time that the definition of integrity was *"keeping one's commitment even after the circumstances have changed."* People will change what they meant, to accommodate what they want, and take no thought at what it will do to their integrity.

The *Body of Christ needs a revival in integrity, character and excellence.* **Character has no power without Godly content.** Content has no power without integrity.

The church is in mass confusion. We are spending more time on appearances and less time on building our content. Leaders have become unfaithful; followers have become unfaithful. The only constant faithful One is GOD!

Appearances aren't the real you. Content is the real you!

It's my prayer that as you go through this book you are going to discover that no matter what the circumstances are, **God will be faithful** to what He has promised. We will laugh, shout and cry together, but at the end we will be convinced to trust God without hesitation. As a matter of fact, God never told you to trust man. He said to love men and trust God!

It is my desire to take you through the Word of God - Genesis to Revelation - and show you all the situations, people and nations where God showed His faithfulness. I will also share my testimony on how faithful God really was to me.

I am hoping that you will take this book and build a passion for God, His church, and for His Word. Everybody fails. When you fail, you will discover God has not failed you.

When you find yourself doing something you thought you would never do, **don't panic** and run away from God; run straight to Him! He's not the one judging you; He is the One that will forgive you.

God is the One leading you back to truth. **I know the church doesn't always walk in love when people make mistakes.** Do not blame God if you have experienced wrong reactions from the church. Don't take out on Him what humans do. Remember, God is not a man. God is not the one pushing you away; He's the source that is pulling you closer. God is the love that's pulling you in. GOD IS LOVE!

"For all have sinned and have fallen short."

"There's none righteous, not one."

We are all a product of "Grace," and if "Grace" got you out the first time, it will get you out again.

Dr. G

Chapter One

GOD
is
FAITHFUL

*H*ave you ever sat down and just thought about God? I don't mean thinking in the way you were raised to think. I'm talking about putting serious thought into who God is and how He really operates. Have you ever studied the character and integrity of God?

The history of mankind reveals the wickedness of human nature. Every person that has ever walked this earth has pursued their fleshly desires and passions at least once during their lifetime. Everyone has made at least one decision based on what they wanted and not what was right for others. Men and women have refused to do what was right in the eyes of God from the beginning of time until now.

We all let God down. Many people do what they want while knowing in their heart it is against God's will.

"There is a way which seemeth right unto a man, but the end thereof are the ways of death." Proverbs 14:12 KJV

"…every inclination…of the human heart was only evil all the time." Genesis 6:5 NIV

This is why my mind is blown away by the majesty of God. No matter how bad we've been to ourselves and to others, God doesn't respond or react in the way we think He would. God's word tells us and history reminds us that God not only receives repentance, He offers forgiveness! This is absolutely crazy. I guess it is true! *God is not a man…! (Numbers 23:19)* This is not normal. God has been anything but normal.

GOD'S NOT NORMAL

God has never done anything normal in my opinion. God is far beyond our mental comprehension. Everything about God - from His works to His instructions - is illogical and irrational to the human mind. We have to move out of the limitations of logical thinking to unlock God's miracle working power. We must stretch our thinking into a limitless world of faith.

We are normal creatures. Everything about us exists in the realm of normal. God is abnormal. No human mind can even attempt to conceive and understand God. That's why we must exercise faith in our movement and response to God.

We are natural beings. Everything we do is within the boundaries of the natural. No man can escape this fact. Mankind has accomplished some pretty incredible things throughout history like flying and space travel. Man was able to go beyond the limits of what is natural because a law of God – aerodynamics, gravity, etc – was discovered. When we surrender to God's laws the natural will give way to the supernatural.

The reason many are not experiencing the supernatural power of God is because they are unwilling to activate His laws - or principles - in their lives. You must shift your thinking from natural to supernatural if you want to experience the miracle power of God! God is not confined to the natural realm… He is SUPERNATURAL! Everything He does will always be *super*.

We must be willing to walk in the "un-natural" in order to see the manifestation of the supernatural such as overflow, prosperity and anointing. This allows God to do what is *natural to Him!*

It is natural for God to bless us, increase us, make us the head and not the tail, to heal us, and deliver us. (Deuteronomy 28)

When I do what "feels" natural or what religion tells us is natural, I force God to become unnatural and withhold His hand of favor, healing and deliverance! This is not what God's natural response is. This is what happens when we lack faith and walk in unbelief. When I do what is unnatural in my flesh God can now do what is natural in the Spirit... RELEASE THE FOG. (The favor of God)

THE NATURAL RESPONSE TO OFFENSE

If someone does us wrong we immediately desire **retaliation, revenge, payback and punishment**. Think about those who have hurt you...people who have stabbed you in the back or have talked about you. If you're like me, you have dreamed and imagined ways to make those who hurt you to pay. The pain they've caused cries for justice. Not so with God! We read stories of people after people, nation after nation defying and rebelling against the plan and purpose of God in the Bible. God always responded in love and forgiveness. God is definitely not moved by what's happening around Him or to Him. He's not reacting to our actions. God stays committed to His purpose over our lives.

The word of God gives us the ability to create a firm foundation of God's love for us and our love for Him. We become better people and can move into the plan of God for our lives when we have clear understanding. Read the verses below and mediate on them.

"Thy mercy, O LORD, is in the heavens; and thy faithfulness reacheth unto the clouds." Psalms 36:5 KJV

"I will sing of the Lord's great love forever; with my mouth I will make your <u>faithfulness</u> known through all generations. I will declare that your love stands firm forever, that you have established <u>your faithfulness</u> in heaven itself. You said, "I have made a covenant with my chosen one, I have sworn to David my servant, 'I will establish your line forever and make your throne firm through all generations.'" The heavens praise your wonders, LORD, your <u>faithfulness too</u>, in the assembly of the holy ones." Psalms 89:1-5 NIV

"My faithful love will be with him, and through my name his horn will be exalted." Psalms 89:24 NIV

"If his sons forsake my law and do not follow my statutes, if they violate my decrees and fail to keep my commands, I will punish their sin with the rod, their iniquity with flogging; but I will not take my love from him, nor will I ever betray my <u>faithfulness</u>." Psalms 89:30-33 NIV

To go further, to dig deeper and to move into a revelation of God's faithfulness, we need to define the word **faithful.**

Webster's Dictionary defines the word "**FAITHFUL**" as

1 keeping faith; maintaining **allegiance; constant; loyal**
2 marked by or showing a strong sense of duty or responsibility; conscientious
3 **accurate; reliable;   full of faith**

Just this one thought should energize us. This one dynamic fact about God should set us at ease with Him. He's not seeking to destroy or punish us. His purpose is to heal us and promote us into His good will.

Facts About God:

1. God has made a covenant (union, partnership) with us.
2. God is loyal and constant.
3. God never breaks His word or His covenant.
4. God takes care of those who walk in agreement to His Word.
5. God is love.
6. God is just.
7. God is Holy.
8. God is all-powerful, all knowing.
9. God is everywhere at every time and in every season.

Promise: *...**God has said, "Never will I leave you; never will I forsake you." Hebrews 13:5 NIV***

Allow this scripture to sink deep into your heart. Let this understanding germinate in your inner spirit and let a harvest of peace and as-surety overtake your mind. **Crises Happen!** No one is exempt from experiencing situations. Bad things happen every day to good people. The truth is life is going to dish it out to you.

Crises and mistakes will happen. When the pressures of life seem to be winning and there's nothing left in you to even pray, remember Hebrews 13:5 **"God will never leave you; never will he forsake you."** Cling, cleave and grab hold to this. In times of despair **we are never alone**. Everyone wants to give up and throw in the towel at some point in life. I have wondered many times why I keep on doing what I'm doing. Do you want to know what truth keeps me going? God is always present helping me, guiding me and encouraging me. If He's doing that for me, He is also doing that for you.

"God is our refuge and strength, an ever-present help in trouble." Psalms 46:1 NIV

Just because you can't feel God or haven't experienced Him in your crisis, doesn't mean He is not working behind the scenes. God is God in spite of what I feel or know. God is working His perfect plan. We are assured that the plans of God are to prosper us, to give us health, to cause us to succeed (Jeremiah 29:11). You must have this confidence that God is faithful to His plan. Guess what? You're in that plan. I'm in that plan. He's working it out even when we cannot feel or see Him.

GOD'S NAME IS NEVER MENTIONED IN THE BOOK OF ESTHER

The name of God is never mentioned **in the book of Esther**; yet all through the book you can sense and see God working His plan behind the scenes.

God was the one orchestrating all those awesome plans. It was God who was setting up the enemy's demise. I've heard it said, *"Satan has a plot, but God has a plan."*

Be encouraged that it is God who works all things out for our good according to His plan and purpose *(Romans 8:28)*. This is a comforting thought to me. I hope it is for you as well. Just as God did in Esther's day, God is still doing today.

We must come to the understanding that the word of God is ALIVE. It's not just a literature book. It's not a history book. It is the breath of God. The **Bible is alive! Everything written in its pages** did happen and is still happening in our lives. Remember, God is working in your immediate situation or circumstance even when you do not feel Him. God is working it out right now!

Search your memories and you will find that God has been behind the scenes working His plans on your behalf and His purposes in all of life's trials and tribulations, for your good...**WOW! What an awesome God He is!**

"And we know that in all things God works for the good of those who love him, who have been called according to his purpose." Romans 8:28 NIV

There are two conditions involved to activate this verse:
    (1) Love God
    (2) Be called according to His **purpose.**

God has set a mandate in His Word so that if we walk according to it, He will make sure that He works all things out for our good. Notice that it doesn't say *that all things will be good at all times*. No, it says that no matter what, if we love God and if we accept our place in His calling, *(Note: we are all called to do something for God)* He's going to work things out for goodness sake. It will be good; trust God!

GOD IS FAITHFUL!

The F.O.G. is evident in so many areas in our lives. There's the F.O.G. (Favor of God.) There's the F.O.G. (Fatherhood of God), and the F.O.G. (Faithfulness of God). The F.O.G. is not just a one-dimensional concept (Favor). Many have preached the F.O.G. message focusing only on favor. Don't get me wrong, favor is awesome and favor is needed. However, the F.O.G.is bigger and moves in all dimensions.

MY PERSONAL EXPERIENCE OF THE FOG:

Who would have ever thought that an Alabama boy, who graduated from high school with a 1.9 G.P.A. and couldn't read very well, would be writing books about God? I serve a miracle-working God! He is definitely the **F.O.G.** to me.

He's been faithful when I was not.

This was the whole reason Paul wrote Romans chapter eight:

"Therefore, there is now no condemnation for those who are in Christ Jesus, because through Christ Jesus the law of the Spirit who gives life has set you free from the law of sin and death.   For what the law was powerless to do because it was weakened by the flesh, God did by sending his own Son in the likeness of sinful flesh to be a sin offering. And so he condemned sin in the flesh, in order that the righteous requirement of the law might be fully met in us, who do not live according to the flesh but according to the Spirit." Romans 8:1-4 NIV

God doesn't choose people by where they are but by where they are going to end up in life. I don't care what you've done - committed adultery, addicted to drugs or alcohol, had an abortion, committed murder, walked in rebellion against a parent - God never picks people on what they're doing but by what they can do and will do.

I call this the law of potential. Potential is not what I've done. Potential is what I haven't done, but can still do. Potential is not where I've been; it's where I haven't been but can still go. Potential isn't what I have; it's what I don't have but can still have. Believe this. You don't have to stay where you are. You don't have to keep living the life you're living. You can change this very day. Maybe you're thinking, how? I will tell you how. Your decisions! Your life can change as fast as you can make a decision. *"Decisions decide most everything in your life."*

The greatest decision you will ever make is to accept Jesus Christ as your Savior and Lord over your life. You can make that decision simply by turning your heart toward Jesus and confessing Him as the Son of God. Believe that He died for your sins and rose from the dead. Confess Him as Lord right now and ask Him to forgive you of your mistakes. When you say this prayer in faith, Jesus forgives you and removes your sins as far as the east is from the west! ***"There shall be no more condemnation."*** For he whom the Son has set free, is free indeed. **You are free!**

WORD OF CAUTION

I didn't say that if you prayed this prayer you wouldn't have to suffer the consequences of bad decisions. Sometimes consequences last longer than we would like and we have to endure them. I've seen a lot of men in prison receive salvation, but they are still serving their sentence. **Why?** They broke the law and have to pay the consequences for their crime. The good news is that now they are not alone. They have been forgiven. Even though they have to serve their sentence, they have been freed from their guilt and condemnation. They will not have to pay for their crimes for eternity.

"Wrong decisions trigger the law of unintended consequences." Dr. Jerry Grillo

These men at one time had to face the sorrow of their wrong doings, and so did we. Now they have the partnership of God and all His resources to help in times of need. So don't misunderstand me. **God is faithful** to His word. It is imperative that you read the Bible and listen with your spirit so that you will have revelation and promise to hold onto in times of difficulties.

Chapter Two

Silence Wrong Voices

*M*any have missed the power and blessings of God simply because they wouldn't walk away from bad influences. I can tell who you are by the company you keep. Your friends are the proof of the person you think you are. I can tell the opinion you have of yourself by who you hang with.

What you're comfortable with is decided by what you can hang with. Take an inventory of those you are comfortable being around. Monitor what your friends do in your presence. Take a moment and observe what's happening in your life. Notice that the same thing is probably happening in your friend's life. Who's pouring into you? Whose voice moves you? Whose mentorship do you seek?

You must recognize that those pouring into you decide what's coming out of you. When I decided to grow and enlarge my territory, I had to discern who was keeping me from enlarging. I realized that if I wanted a different future I had to have a different present. This is the most powerful statement you will ever need to hear; "Not every person connected to you is *good for you*." You can change your life when you change your friends. Think for just a moment...friends are usually the ones who try to talk you out of change. If you announce that you are going on a diet, you will get a phone call from one of your friends who wanted to let you know they baked your favorite cake. Most of the time, when you decide to change, it will be at the expense of those you've chosen to run with. Let them go! I promise you. Your next season of friends will be way better than the ones you have in your present season.

My greatest enemy as a youth pastor was the wrong kids my youth would hang out with. I used to dread when school started. Summer break meant the teens would be around positive influences. They would come to youth church and have zeal and hunger for the things of God. Then school would start. Those same kids who were worshipping and excited about the things of God started looking dead and disoriented in the presence of God. What happened? They began to take on the attitude and atmosphere of those they were hanging out with at school.

I realized that we were going to have to build a different kind of peer pressure in order to win this battle. We were going to have to change the mentality of the youth. We needed to establish a partnership opportunity for those who were in the Kingdom. I began to monitor the attitude and connections the gang members were perpetrating, and, I started a youth group gang. I called it the **"Soul Patrol."** Yeah, I know it sounds corny now, but back in the eighties it worked. I called it positive peer pressure.

If someone walked up to my youth in school and made fun of them for blessing their food at the lunch table, my youth would stand up with pride and confidence and say boldly, *"Absolutely, I'm praying. Why, are you too cool to do it?"*

They would walk down the hallway with their Bibles. If someone tried to embarrass them, they wouldn't hide their Bible in shame. They would say with confidence *"WHERE'S YOURS?"*

Positive Peer Pressure... when you stand up against the flow of normal and walk faithful to God's word, expect God's faithfulness to produce favor. Sometimes you may have to walk alone, but only for a season.

Let's look at an example of someone who stood up against peer pressure and faced great odds. God favored Him for it. This example lived many, many years ago. He was in the first generations of humans. We can find this example in

Genesis chapters five through nine. This person was named NOAH.

Noah's name means nuwach (noo'-akh); *a primitive root; to rest, i.e. settle down;   (to dwell, stay, let fall, place, alone, with-draw, give comfort, etc.)*

Pay attention to the meaning of Noah's name; notice that Noah's name shows us that he was a man of rest. He was settled. His name bears the mark that he was probably a peaceful and good man, one who didn't cause a lot of grief and was always in good spirits. The Bible says that he was a righteous man.

Noah was a good man, but he lived among people who were wicked, rebellious and involved in all kinds of sexual sins. They were a people running out of control. Man had become a cesspool of lust, hatred, and all other kinds of sin, but Noah stayed peaceful and restful.

Noah stayed to himself. The best way to keep from falling into the trap of **peer-pressure** is to stay away from those who can pressure you to fall. Be comfortable with you. Be true to yourself. Don't allow the popularity of others to stop you from being popular with God. Pleasing people is costly. Pleasing God is always rewarding in the end.

Noah had made up his mind to stay away from the God-haters. He decided to keep his altar and his life connected to God's ways instead of man's ways.

"The LORD saw how great the wickedness of the human race had become on the earth, and that every inclination of the thoughts of the human heart was only evil all the time. The LORD regretted that he had made human beings on the earth, and his heart was deeply troubled. So the LORD said, "I will wipe from the face of the earth the human race

I have created-and with them the animals, the birds and the creatures that move along the ground-for I regret that I have made them." Genesis 6:5-7 NIV

"Now the earth was corrupt in God's sight and was full of violence. God saw how corrupt the earth had become, for all the people on earth had corrupted their ways." Genesis 6:11-12 NIV

"But Noah found favor in the eyes of the LORD... Noah was a righteous man, blameless among the people of his time, and he walked faithfully with God." Genesis 6:8-9 NIV

Mankind had saddened the heart of God. Humanity had turned out terribly wicked. God said, *even the thoughts and intent of man's heart was wicked continually, not just for a moment.* Mankind had become persistently rebellious against God's will.

This is where we begin to see the real plan and nature of God. God could have just wiped out mankind. He could have decided right then and there that man wasn't worth the investment. Just as you think the enemy is gaining an upper hand on God, God punches back with His nature and plan. *His love is far bigger than His disappointments.*

God looked down and saw what man had become. God was considering in his heart to wipe out mankind completely. God said, *"I will destroy mankind and every living thing on the earth."* All of a sudden the narration turns. The hurt turned into mercy and love. God couldn't ignore one man who decided not to give into the intentions of His heart...a man who burned offerings to God...the God that Adam had taught about generation after generation. This one man, Noah puts a wrench in the wheel of judgment. *God can't ignore an offering! God won't ignore your worship! God will never ignore your sacrifice!*

God's heart was turned and He could not completely wipe out mankind. **"Noah found favor."** Noah found the **F.O.G**. (Favor of God) and the **F.O.G. (Faithfulness of God**) found Noah.

Just think how easy it could have been for God to erase all His troubles with one word of destruction. Think about it. Jesus would have never had to suffer. He would have never been crucified. All God needed to do was wipe out man and that would have been judgment. Yet there was one man named Noah who had not succumbed to the sins of the populace. He was a just, quiet, peaceful man living the best he could for God. God saw Noah and was reminded that no matter how bad mankind seemed, there was someone who walked in goodness. He would spare mankind as long as there was hope.

> Noah Found Favor in the Eyes of The Lord!

In Genesis chapter three, God told the serpent that a seed was coming that would crush the serpent's head. If God had destroyed mankind, those words would have been void. We know that heaven and earth will pass away, but God's word will never die.

God told Noah to build an **ARK**! It was going to rain! God was about to create His *great escape*! He was about to become Noah's **"way maker."** God was faithful to Noah because Noah stayed faithful to God. I love this because it shows that God spared mankind because one man stayed loyal. This one decision spared many in the future. Don't ever think that your stand for what is right, for truth and for God isn't making a difference. Not only did God spare Noah, He also spared all of his family. God took care of what was connected to Noah. God was so merciful that He even allowed time for Noah to reach others and bring them into the **ARK** with him.

Noah preached for 120 years, but no one came into the **ARK** except Noah and his family. The **ARK** was a type of Christ. It was the place where you would be spared from judgment. As long as Noah stayed in the Ark, he and his family would not feel the pain of judgment. Just imagine sitting in that boat and listening to all the people screaming, *"Noah! Let us in!"* All Noah could do was cling to the **ARK** (Jesus). Jesus is our **ARK**! When we come to Him and enter into His covenant, we will miss the judgment of God and be protected by the **ARK** of His blood. I believe that God will always spare our family when we live according to His Word. We will find **FAVOR! God was faithful to Noah, and He's going to be faithful to you!**

Chapter Three

GOD IS MOVED BY FAITH

"When God made his promise to Abraham, since there was no one greater for him to swear by, he swore by himself, saying, "I will surely bless you and give you many descendants." And so after waiting patiently, Abraham received what was promised." Hebrews 6:13-15 NIV

"By faith Abraham, when called to go to a place he would later receive as his inheritance, obeyed and went, even though he did not know where he was going. By faith he made his home in the Promised Land like a stranger in a foreign country; he lived in tents, as did Isaac and Jacob, who were heirs with him of the same promise. For he was looking forward to the city with foundations, whose architect and builder is God. And by faith even Sarah, who was past childbearing age, was enabled to bear children because she considered him faithful who had made the promise. And so from this one man, and he as good as dead, came descendants as numerous as the stars in the sky and as countless as the sand on the seashore." Hebrews 11:8-12 NIV

"By faith Abraham, when God tested him, offered Isaac as a sacrifice. He who had embraced the promises was about to sacrifice his one and only son, even though God had said to him, "It is through Isaac that your offspring will be reckoned." Abraham reasoned that God could even raise the dead, and so in a manner of speaking, he did receive Isaac back from death." Hebrews 11:17-19 NIV

God has never been driven by the needs of others. The world is full of the needy. If God was moved by pain and suffering then there would never be any on the earth. God isn't moved by what we are going through; He's moved by our reactions to what we are going through. Need doesn't move God... faith moves God!

- Faith isn't a feeling!
- Faith isn't motivation.
- Faith isn't how I shout.
- Faith is revealed in my actions. Words don't prove faith! Actions prove my faith.

"What does it profit, my brethren, if someone says he has faith but does not have works? Can faith save him? If a brother or sister is naked and destitute of daily food, and one of you says to them, "Depart in peace, be warmed and filled," but you do not give them the things which are needed for the body, what does it profit? Thus also faith by itself, if it does not have works, is dead. But someone will say, "You have faith, and I have works." James 2:14 -18 NKJV

- Why faith?
- Why does God require faith?
- Why does God need us to use our faith?
- Why does He place such an important focus on faith?

I'm sure you have asked these questions at least once in your life. I have asked myself these questions many times. Faith is heaven's currency. Faith is the proof you've placed your trust in something bigger than you.

How is God going to really know we are persuaded He is who He says He is? *By our faith*! We prove our trust when we walk by faith.

What is faith? Many have attempted to explain faith, so I am going to try to explain it the way I see it. Some have said that it's confidence in God; others have said it's a persuasion. Some have said faith believes.

All of these are true, but I believe it's more! I believe that faith is more than confidence. Confidence is a good thing for sure, but confidence is a feeling. Confidence increases when something or someone builds our feelings and security. Confidence has to be motivated. I like thinking of faith as being more than just confidence.

Faith is a persuasion. Faith is not just believing that God can. The easiest thing to do is believe that God can. He's God. He's the Author and Finisher of everything. God is all-powerful, all-knowing and everywhere. God can absolutely heal us, save us, bless us and deliver us from our enemies. God hung every star and created the universe, light, plants and every living thing just by the power of His words. He's God, and He can do all things.

"For He spoke, and it was done; He commanded, and it stood fast." Psalms 33:9 KJV

"By faith we understand that the universe was formed at God's command, so that what is seen was not made out of what was visible." Hebrews 11:3 NIV

Real faith moves past the thought that God can and into the reality that GOD WILL!

<u>Faith believes God will!</u>

Let's go deeper. Faith does not just believe God will but believes in His eternal power. Time doesn't hinder His ability to move. God isn't going to heal me or going to bless me. Faith says, "He's already healed me. God's already blessed me."

Abraham Is Called The Father Of Faith

We are created with the power of choice so that makes us easy targets for the enemy to attack. Abraham didn't just believe God in times when everything seemed to be okay or in times of great victories. Abraham believed God when everything else was failing. No matter how hard he tried, he couldn't seem to produce a child.

Abraham was in his seventies when God promised him a son. God didn't fulfill his promise to Abraham until he was almost one hundred years old. As a matter of fact, the word of God says that God waited. God waited until Abraham was as good as dead in his natural potential to produce seed and Sarah his wife had reached the season in her life that she was unable to bear children. Why did God take so long to fulfill His promise?

The only answer I can offer is that faith must be tested. Delayed promises force us to reveal if we trust God. God always seems to assign death to a seed promise. We must understand that when God gives us a promise time will be scheduled to it; time for that seed to die and reveal its full potential. Faith is required from all of us. We must believe not only when God is speaking but also while we are waiting, watching and praying. The seed must die so that it can live!

No matter what time God chooses to fulfill His promise, you must believe He will fulfill it! That's the faith that creates great prosperity, great healings and great testimonies. Believe that God will be faithful to what He has promised. Abraham believed this. He didn't allow his situation to dictate his belief system. He rested on the words of the Lord.

Faith isn't faith until you can pass the test of time… You must pass the test of difficulties, the test of waiting on God to come through and the test of loss while in waiting! God took twenty-six years to fulfill a promise to Abraham. God waited until there was no human potential to be factored into the equation. If there was any human intervention to your miracle then how would you know God did it? God has to allow all human possibilities and variables to be dealt with before He will manifest His promises. There has to be no human part in the performance of any miracle from God. There has to be this overwhelming feeling that if God doesn't do it, it isn't going to get done. Let me put it this way. The only part you will play in your miracle is to not waiver in your belief and faith that God will come through. Maybe you're thinking right now, will He? Yes, He WILL!

Your Faith Will Be Tested

You must be willing to reach seasons of drought and emptiness for God to be the source of your miracle. Empty is opportunity and loss means more! It's at the time you feel as good as dead that God will walk into your situation and give you the very word of encouragement that's going to bring you out and take you into your next season of promotion.

By faith, when Abraham was tested and believed God, it was credited to him as righteousness. Get a good grasp of this. Good works or deeds do not obtain righteousness. That's not to say that works and deeds aren't a part of the Christian walk. The word says that he was credited with righteousness because he took God at His Word and nothing or no one was going to persuade Abraham otherwise.

One more thing to think about:

What about Sarah? She not only was required to have faith but she had to be the one to carry the seed of promise. Sarah had to enter a higher level of faith. Sarah not only had to believe it, she had to conceive it. The word says that we need to have faith in our heart. There is no such thing as head faith; there is only heart faith.

There is no way you can understand how God is going to heal your cancer, pay a bill that you have no natural funds to pay, or bring home your child who has been away from the Lord. Your mind doesn't possess the ability to understand God, but your heart does. Your mind says how... your heart says I believe! No human is capable of understanding how miracles happen. That's why they are called miracles. The spirit of man has the power to believe without understanding how.

> **With God Empty Is Opportunity And Loss Means More!**

SPIRITUAL CONCEPTION

Sarah had to have the heart to conceive. Here are some steps that we need to be able to walk through to reach our promised blessings...

4 STEPS FOR OUTLIVING MY DEAD SEASON

1. You must first **believe it**. That's faith. Faith is now; faith is the substance of things hoped for,

and the evidence of things not seen. Hebrews11:1 KJV

2. You must be able to **conceive it**. The word conception comes from the word conceive. When the visitors came to Abraham's house one evening, they told him that Sarah would be pregnant. Sarah laughed when she heard this, and the Lord asked Abraham, "Why is your wife laughing?" Sarah couldn't conceive in her mind that she was going to be pregnant. After all, it had been twenty-six years and there still was no promised child. The Lord was going to perform the miracle, but waited another year. He had to get Sarah ready to conceive. Conception is the ability to see your promised blessing and carry it internally.

3. You must **receive it**. When you can **believe it** and **conceive it,** you will be ready to **receive it**.

4. You will **achieve it**.

Abraham's faith produced his son Isaac. Isaac's name means laughter. No matter how long it takes for God to produce His promise, you will be filled with so much *joy* and *excitement* when it comes. You will be laughing, shouting and dancing. You won't be able to hide the promise. The joy that you will exude will be so powerful it will actually cause others to follow your God.

Your praise and worship is different when you survive a dead season. I love to watch people who stay focused through their crises and then watch them praise when God's promises come to pass. I'm telling you, Faith in God will produce the **faithfulness of God**.

Chapter 4

Obey Godly Instructions

Another word for obedience is submission.

What is submission?

Webster's dictionary defines submission as *"the quality or condition of being submissive; resignation; obedience; meekness a) the act of submitting something to another for decision, consideration, etc. b) something thus submitted, as an article or photograph to a publisher c) Law, an agreement whereby parties to a dispute submit the matter to arbitration and agree to be bound by the decision."*

To be a submissive person you must know whom you are being submissive too. There must be a confidence and trust in the person you have chosen to be submitted to as well as what you are being asked to do.

To be submissive you must come into agreement with the person set over you. Contrary to popular opinion, you don't have to be in agreement when you are in submission. A spirit of meekness is applied to your heart. You may not like what you are being asked to do, but no matter what, you submit!

SERVING CAN BE GREATER THAN LEADING

The willingness to submit carries with it the most wonderful anointing. There is a special grace on servants. The power of the submitted is sometimes greater than the one who is leading.

Those who decide to obey the instructions of those in authority over them benefit from the reward of the instruction but not the consequences if the instruction caused a wrong result.

This is strong! **Get this!** You are rewarded for obeying the man of God and released from the penalty if the decision was wrong. God will not hold you responsible because you were in submission. You are in line for the blessing, and out of line for the consequences.

Christians need to learn the art of trusting God and submitting to His will and word. We want to do everything our own way too often.

Christianity isn't an independent walk. It is a dependent walk. God wants us to depend on Him. He wants to be our supplier. He wants us to trust Him to take care of us every day and not worry about tomorrow.

Abraham and Isaac learned to walk in complete submission.

The Test of all Tests!

God came to Abraham and asked him to sacrifice Isaac - his only son - on the mountain.

"Then God said, "Take your son, your only son, whom you love-Isaac-and go to the region of Moriah. Sacrifice him there as a burnt offering on a mountain I will show you." Genesis 22:2 NIV

God was requiring back from Abraham what He so generously gave him. Why would God put Abraham through such a painful experience? Why would God give him a gift and ask for it back?

Abraham doesn't even offer an argument to God. What's wrong with Abraham?

What about Isaac? He allows his father the access necessary to tie him up and put a knife to his throat.

Submission begins when agreement ends. Submission isn't agreement. Sometimes you must do what goes against your logical thinking to be in submission.

...ILLOGICAL   INSTRUCTION,   BUT   NOT IMPOSSIBLE...

Your willingness to obey an instruction will promote you to the next season of your life. Almost every instruction from God will be illogical but not impossible. Think about this for a moment...

- It was illogical for Noah to build an ark, but not impossible.
- It was illogical for Moses to lead millions out of slavery and through the wilderness, but not impossible.
- It was illogical for Daniel to survive the lions' den, but not impossible.

Allow me to dig deeper into this. Let's move from the mind of Abraham and move into the mind of God. Abraham knew this was an illogical instruction, but believed in a God who could and would do the impossible.

Abraham had been requested to sacrifice his son, Isaac, on Mount Moriah. He waited so long for the fulfillment of this promise that it is almost absurd for Abraham to even comply with God's request. Abraham had such an awesome love for God that he didn't even offer up an argument. Isn't this the man that pleaded with God to spare Sodom and Gomorrah? But here, with his own son, he doesn't even try to offer a substitute. What was the Lord really after? I believe that God wasn't really looking for a human sacrifice, but a willing heart totally submitted to trusting God, even to the point of surrendering what you love the most. After all, isn't God going to be required to do just that for us? God didn't have anybody hiding in the wings to save His sacrifice.

The difference between seasons in your life is an instruction.

God was testing Abraham's love and commitment. After all, he was going to be the father of many nations. God knew if he wasn't able to sow his seed, he would never be able to collect, or reap his harvest. The same applies for you and me. When God asks for our seed it's not the seed that He has in mind; **it's our harvest.**

Can't you picture this man packing for his journey? Can you imagine him explaining to Sarah what the Lord was requesting of them? Sarah may have responded, "God wants what? He's asking you to do what? Kill the promise seed! You've got to be kidding me! We waited so long, are you sure Abraham?"

"Yes," replied her husband.

"So be it. Do whatever you see fit." What an awesome wife Sarah was to be willing to let go and trust her husband. Let's get an in-depth look at the scriptures.

"Early the next morning Abraham got up and loaded his donkey. He took with him two of his servants and his son Isaac. When he had cut enough wood for the burnt offering, he set out for the place God had told him about. On the third day Abraham looked up and saw the place in the distance. He said to his servants, "Stay here with the

donkey while I and the boy go over there. We will worship and then we will come back to you." Genesis 22:3-5 NIV

This story is a type and shadow of God and Jesus. Notice the first thing Abraham had to do was take a journey to Mount Moriah. This is in reference to the journey the Lord Jesus had to take to be born, trained and live as a human.

Second, when Abraham reached his destination, it was on the third day. Three is a significant number. The number three in the Hebrew means power or resurrection.

Third, in verse five we see a donkey in the story. We can recall that Jesus tells his disciples to go to Jerusalem and find a donkey tied up. Jesus told them to tell the owner that the Lord was in need of it. Jesus rode into the city riding a donkey and the people cried out, "Hosanna."

What symbolism!

God was foreshadowing in the Old Testament what would actually take place two thousand years later in the New Testament.

There was a professor in Bible College who used to say *"you will never be able to understand the New Testament unless you grasp an understanding of the Old Testament."* Never let someone convince you that you are not supposed to live by, or will ever need to live by, the words of the Old Testament. **That is a lie!**

Abraham's words to his servants give you a clue that he had enough faith in God that they would be back and not just him alone.

"...We will worship and then we will come back to you," with the emphasis on the word we! Abraham was confessing his results to his servants for his obedience. He was saying, "I'm going to be submissive; I'm going to sow this seed!

Nevertheless, I'm not coming back empty handed. **WE WILL BE BACK!** If I kill him, **God will raise** him!"

Abraham had faith in God…this God that he had become familiar with. Abraham had built a trust in God because he was a man that talked (prayed) to God often. He possessed the mind of God and the attitude of God. He was going to be obedient to this Jehovah and trust Him in total obedience.

Abraham wasn't going to hold anything back from worshipping God. He wasn't about to do anything or allow anyone to stop him from showing God how much he loved Him.

What about you? What are you holding back that keeps you from walking in total obedience? What are you allowing to stay in your life that God has been requiring you to sow?

We will never possess the blessings of Abraham as long as we continue to hold on to the things that God has been requiring us to sow. God is testing us, just as He did Abraham, to see what we are willing to walk away from. Abraham would have loved Isaac more than the Word of God if he had walked away from Isaac. We must love God's Word more than anything else in our lives. This is encouraging. God is able to do the impossible in our lives when we love God's word more than anything. All we need to do is believe, conceive and receive!

Just let your mind wander right now and visualize this with me. Abraham was acting in blind, total submission to God in every step up the mountain of trial. Every rock, every boulder and every weed he had to remove to take him closer to his offering. All this would not have been possible without the will to be and act in submission.

No matter how hard we try, we cannot desensitize this story. Don't think for one moment that Abraham wasn't fighting the same mental battle that you and I fight every time we set out to obey God. There is no way any of us can experience the blessings of what Abraham experienced if we aren't willing to submit. We must decide to move against our own reasoning, fears and worries.

I can imagine in my mind that Abraham would occasionally look over at his son and feel light headed as his heart began to beat with the pain. I am a father, and I could not imagine having to sow this kind of seed. The love for his son had to be pulling at the very core of his reasoning and rationality. I know he had to be thinking that this was absolutely crazy…absurd! No matter what was going through Abraham's mind, he kept moving toward the will of God. Isn't that what we should do also? We are to keep moving to complete God's will even while our emotions are tormenting us. No matter what we're thinking, just keep moving toward the completion of God's instruction.

Of course, Abraham's mind was going through all the steps of sacrifice. He was screaming with the pain that was tearing at the core of his being, crying in his heart and asking the questions that all of us ask... **"Can I do it; can I bring myself to kill what I love so much? Do I really love God that much? Will I succeed or fail? Oh, God help me! I need you in this hour of trial."**

Let me interject a thought here. God never said a word after he gave Abraham the test. Why? The teacher doesn't talk *when the student is taking a test.* If the teacher has to speak during the test and explain what is going on, then you haven't really learned anything. The time to learn something in life is when you are living on top of the mountain. Take the time necessary to prepare yourself for the test when everything is going good. Get into the Word of God and learn what the Lord needs you to learn so that you can pass the test! When you are in a hard place, perplexed and wondering why you can't hear from God, just remember this... maybe you are taking a test! Just hang on and **pass the test.** Rewards come after the test, not during.

Let's not leave out the son. What about Isaac? He is at an age where he can oppose Abraham. What if Abraham gets to the place and Isaac says no? What if Isaac was unwilling to go through this insane idea?

When they reached the place to build the offering, Isaac asked Abraham where the sacrifice was.

"Isaac spoke up and said to his father Abraham, "Father?" "Yes, my son?" Abraham replied. "The fire and wood are here," Isaac said, "but where is the lamb for the burnt offering? Abraham answered, "God himself will provide the lamb for the burnt offering, my son. "... Genesis 22:7-8 NIV

Abraham kept the faith even at the end of his journey. *"God himself will provide the lamb."* Stop for a moment and let these words work their way into your spirit. Hear the prophetic words in this. Just the first part makes me shiver... **"God Himself."**

"God Himself." This is more than just two words. This is prophetic. God has always been in the supplying business. Abraham brought his only son, but God had no intentions on taking Isaac from Abraham. God only wanted to see if Abraham would give up what He loved to obey God's voice. This is what sacrifices means. It means giving up something you love in your present season, to embrace something much larger in your next season. One son offered, created a harvest of many sons that eventually turned into nations. God stepped in at the final moment and provided a ram for the sacrifice that day.

Thousands of years in the future, God Himself provided again. On a hill called Golgotha, God Himself was crucified. The sacrifice was Jesus. He was placed on the cross for you and me.

"When they reached the place God had told him about, Abraham built an altar there and arranged the wood on it. He bound his son Isaac and laid him on the altar, on top of the wood. Then he reached out his hand and took the knife to slay his son. But the angel of the LORD called out to him from heaven, "Abraham! Abraham!" "Here I am," he replied. "Do not lay a hand on the boy," he said. "Do not do anything to him. Now I know that you fear God, because you have not withheld from me your son, your only son." Abraham looked up and there in a thicket he saw a ram caught by its horns. He went over and took the ram and sacrificed it as a burnt offering instead of his son. So Abraham called that place The LORD Will Provide. And to this day it is said, "On the mountain of the LORD it will be provided." Genesis 22:9-14 NIV

I believe Isaac shows us what kind of children we should be with the father. Isaac never lifts a finger to stop his father. He allows Abraham to tie him up, put him on the wood and watches as his father draws the knife for the kill. What an obedient son. Isaac not only represents Jesus, but he also represents you and me. He was a living sacrifice. He had to choose to let his father do what he needed to do to fulfill the Father's purpose.

That is exactly what we do when we choose to obey the Lord's will in our lives. When we fulfill His purposes and not ours, we will see the **faithfulness of God** present.

JUST BECAUSE YOU DON'T SEE IT, DOESN'T MEAN GOD ISN'T DOING SOMETHING!

Every step up that mountain of **uncertainty,** trial, obedience and sacrifice, a ram was climbing at the same pace on the other side. As long as he kept climbing, he would crash right into his provision. Let me give you the scripture that made Abraham shout out the F.O.G...faithfulness of God.

"The angel of the LORD called to Abraham from heaven a second time and said, "I swear by myself, declares the LORD, that because you have done this and have not withheld your son, your only son, I will surely bless you and make your descendants as numerous as the stars in the sky and as the sand on the seashore. Your descendants will take possession of the cities of their enemies, and through your offspring all nations on earth will be blessed, because you have obeyed me." Genesis 22:15-18 NIV

Total submission to the instructions of God will produce the faithfulness of God in your life just as it did for Abraham. God is, and will always be, at the end of your submission. He will not let you perish in your submission.

If you are in a spiritual or physical struggle right now, **don't give up and don't quit!** Set your face toward heaven and trust God. He is able to get you out. I promise this, you will not come out empty handed.

Endurance is a qualifier!

"And let us not be weary in well doing: for in due season we shall reap, if we faint not." Galatians 6:9 KJV

Chapter 5

Where Have The Servants Gone In God's House?

"...The LORD be exalted, who delights in the well-being of his <u>servant.</u>" My tongue will proclaim your righteousness, your praises all day long." Psalms 35:27-28 NIV

"Truly I am your <u>servant,</u> LORD; I serve you just as my mother did; you have freed me from my chains. I will sacrifice a thank offering to you and call on the name of the LORD. I will fulfill my vows to the LORD in the presence of all his people, in the courts of the house of the LORD--in your midst, Jerusalem. Praise the LORD." Psalms 116:16-19 NIV

The word **"servant,"** or **"bondservant,"** is not a word we hear much about in our culture. Most of us are conditioned to make everything about us. Rightfully so, everything we watch and see on billboards, TV shows and even in some churches promote an *"all about me"* attitude.

Our civilization has embraced a selfish and "take care of me first" mentality. I am constantly being bombarded on Facebook and Twitter with videos of people being beat up while crowds stand by and watch, videotaping and laughing. We are desensitizing the next generation on the power of serving others.

Caring and reaching out to those who need us is becoming a thing of the past. It has become harder and harder, as a spiritual leader, to get anyone to do anything at any time to serve God's interests. I hear often, *"**Pastor we just don't have time to**...school activities...home responsibilities... and work; there's just no more time on the clock for the church."*

Some people try to say that the church is separate from God's interests. This is simply not truth. The church is **God's design, not man's**. We have added our thoughts and perceptions to the organization, but the church was God's plan. He expects us to be as focused on His house as we are on ours.

A deeper walk with God requires...
- Serving
- Sacrifice
- Willingness

A BRIEF HISTORY OF A BONDSERVANT

*In Bible times when the master of a house or plantation would let slaves go free, whether it was for friendship or the year of Jubilee, if the slave chose to come back and stay in and under his master's care, then he wasn't just an ordinary slave he became a **"Bondservant."***

The master would take him over to the doorpost and the slave would put his ear on the door jam. The master would take a sharp object, mark the ear, and put an earring in it. This would signify that he wasn't just a slave; he was a bondservant who chose to stay and serve by his own will.

The word servant appears five hundred fifteen times in the Bible. Serving wasn't a bad word like it is today. People think they have to be compensated for anything they do for another. The greatest seed you can sow is the seed of serving. All of us are called to serve in God's house. Servant simply means to WORK! We must do something more than just attend.

Someone once said, *"No one whose name is worth remembering, ever lived a life of ease."* Nowhere in the word of God do we read anything that even gives us the hint that life is easy or work free. If we want to see our home, our occupation, and our church life fruitful then we must bind together and serve the purposes of God. That purpose is to build a church that will, **"Make the Devil Pay!"**

I am the founder and Bishop of The Favor Center Church in Hickory, North Carolina. The most frustrating thing to me is when I have to beg and plead with people to serve. Oh, they will come forward to be seen in the **"limelight,"** but when it comes time to serve, they will have all kinds of reason why they can't. When you ask someone to do something that puts them in the front they are quick to say okay, but don't ask them to serve in the nursery or in the secret places of the church where few get to see them. The answers will be all kinds of excuses. Some even sign up to serve but don't show up. This has to be addressed because God is not going to favor you if you are not serving in His house.

Don't misunderstand me. I'm not saying sheep are lazy and won't work. They will work...at their jobs, their homes or to make sure that everything for their personal needs are accommodated. They will even stay up all night to make a profit. Ask them why they were not in church and you will get many reasons as to why. They stayed home to make sure the yard was mowed, cars washed and they are rested up for the next day.

Try to instruct them as their Pastor and they look at you with a smug and a self-assured look and say, *"don't preach legalism to me."* Well excuse us for caring enough about church and the Christian faith to question the attendance and attitudes of those God has placed us over!

Why is it that "so called" God-fearing Christians will stay home on mid-week service night to make sure their personal life is taken care of? I believe it's a shame when a church has three hundred in attendance on Sunday morning but won't even break one hundred during a mid -week service.

Allow me to drive this a **bit further.** There is Monday, Tuesday, Thursday, Friday, and Saturday, yet it will be the night we have **"Mid -Week"** that they decide to have family night. Please, stop saying you are about the Kingdom of God. The only kingdom you are actually for is your own.

People have lost respect and understanding for the corporate anointing. I'm not trying to throw rain on your parade, but if we don't put the church back in perspective and back in priority, we are going to miss a revival of His Presence.

NO ONE SUCCEEDS ALONE

No pastor can build a church by himself. Churches can't pay everybody. We need the sheep to start focusing on the church again. Walk around your church and open your eyes. Look around and see what needs to be done and don't wait for someone to do it...you do it. You don't need a spiritual calling to clean the bathrooms, vacuum the carpet or pick up the area around the church. You don't have to wait for some divine revelation to fall from Heaven to be a servant. If you are looking for a word from God, open your ears and listen. Your pastors and leadership have been asking for help. I believe that those who can help and won't, are going to face a hard reality in the end.

Don't attend everyone else's Bible studies when your local church is offering one. Don't go and engage yourself in helping other churches **until you are fulfilling** what you're supposed to do in your church. God didn't plant you in the church down the street. He planted you in the church you are attending right now. You and I can only produce a harvest if we remain planted in the soil. If you keep trying to place and replace yourself in every other field, you will never develop good strong Biblical roots. Without a good root system your harvest will never come.

SERVANTHOOD IS NOT A CUSS WORD!

Serving, and being a servant, will produce the **"Faithfulness of God."** We find such a person who went beyond just what was expected of her in the word of God. She was the very person who was chosen to own the goods she was serving. Her name was Rebecca.

"Abraham was now very old, and the LORD had blessed him in every way. He said to the senior servant in his household, the one in charge of all that he had, "Put your hand under my thigh. I want you to swear by the LORD, the God of heaven and the God of earth, that you will not get a wife for my son from the daughters of the Canaanites, among whom I am living, but will go to my country and my own relatives and get a wife for my son Isaac." Genesis 24:1-4 NIV

"Then the servant left, taking with him ten of his master's camels, loaded with him all kinds of good things from his master. He set out for Aram Naharaim and made his way to the town of Nahor. He had the camels kneel down near the well outside the town; it was toward evening, the time the women go out to draw water. Then he prayed, " LORD, God of my master Abraham, make me successful today, and show kindness to my master Abraham. See, I am standing beside this spring, and the daughters of the townspeople are coming out to draw water. May it be that when I say to a young woman, 'Please let down your jar that I may have a drink,' and she says, 'Drink, and I'll water your camels too'--let her be the one you have chosen for your servant Isaac. By this I will know that you have shown kindness to my master." Before he had finished praying, Rebekah came out with her jar on her shoulder... The woman was very beautiful, a virgin; no man had ever slept with her. She went down to the spring, filled her jar and came up again." Genesis 24:10-16 NIV

Isaac is a type and shadow of Jesus and Rebekah is a type of the church.   Abraham sent ten camels full of **good stuff** with his servants. Who was this stuff for? Not for the servants and not for Rebekah's family. No, this good stuff was held in reserve for the bride of Isaac. When was the bride going to be able to take her place and receive her good stuff? When she accepted her invitation to come!

WILLINGNESS IS THE KEY TO UNLOCKING SACRIFICE

When Are We Going To Experience The Manifestation Of Our Increase?

When we are willing to…
(1) accept the invitation to come to Jesus.
(2) serve the purposes of the Father.
(3) leave everything to follow Jesus.

The servants of Abraham were tired and thirsty when they reached Mesopotamia. They stopped by a well and noticed a damsel. Her name was Rebekah.

I love verse twelve. The servant of Abraham stopped and prayed. This prayer alone shows how much he was dedicated and loyal to his leader.

"… " LORD, God of my master Abraham, make me successful today, and show kindness to my master Abraham. See, I am standing beside this spring, and the daughters of the townspeople are coming out to draw water. May it be that when I say to a young woman, 'Please let down your jar that I may have a drink,' and she says, 'Drink, and I'll water your camels too'--let her be the one you have chosen for your servant Isaac. By this I will know that you have shown kindness to my master." Genesis 24:12-14 NIV

Monitor closely what the servant prayed… *"Lord …make me **successful today**."*

We are never going to achieve and accomplish anything for God if we don't pray daily for Godly success. This prayer wasn't for them; they were on a mission for the master and they desired to be successful for their master's sake.

The church will see the cloud (presence of God) when the body of Christ becomes driven by their desire to fulfill the **purposes** of God more than the desires of self. We need to become a church that will accommodate to the Cloud and not to the crowd. Crowd focused churches spend hours working on events and programs. They want to squeeze a service into a small window of time. I'm not against a time schedule or planning. However, I am against pleasing people more than pleasing and obeying the laws and principles of God.

> *The church needs to cater to the CLOUD and not the CROWD!*

Secondly, the servant put a test on the bride…the test was sacrifice.

SERVANT-HOOD Always Requires Sacrifice

"May it be that when I say to a young woman, 'Please let down your jar that I may have a drink,' and she says, 'Drink, and I'll water your camels too'--let her be the one you have chosen for your servant Isaac. By this I will know that you have shown kindness to my master."" Genesis 24:14 NIV

This was not just a test of willingness; it was also a test of character. What kind of attitude would Rebecca have while doing the test?

Think for a moment and imagine yourself being assigned to get water for your family. This was Rebecca's responsibility.

Rebecca had just finished her daily chores and was tired when she was asked to serve someone she did not even know. *What would your response be?* After all, these strangers from a different country were not her responsibility. Rebekah's response passed the test.

Rebekah is amazing. She not only takes care of her personal responsibilities, she takes care of Abraham's servants and offers to take care of all ten of their camels while they are drinking and resting.

She is running back and forth filling the trough with buckets of water. Do you have any idea how much water a camel can drink? Rebekah had ten camels to satisfy. This woman had to carry gallons and gallons of water to the trough.

Her act and attitude of servant hood required more from her than just a few minutes of work. She used an amazing amount of effort, time and strength. She must have been beyond exhausted.

However, imagine her as she looks over every camel and notices all the good stuff they are loaded down with. Maybe she felt the fur and silk and imagined herself in them. She saw the gold, silver and jewels and might have imagined how beautiful they would look on her.

She never one time considered that the camels, and all of the stuff she was taking care of, were actually going to be hers. God will be faithful to us when we serve the purposes of God and we are willing to work to fulfill His cause.

There is a difference between doing the work of a servant and having the ***attitude of a servant***. One is an outward response to an external gain; the other is the fiber of what we are made of. You will eventually become frustrated when you are just doing the work of a servant and don't have the character of a servant. Your true colors will always be revealed when you are treated like a servant.

SERVANT WORKER -VS- A SERVANT'S ATTITUDE!

There are many who will only serve for the promotion they can gain. These people only see increase and success, blind to the struggle and wisdom it takes to be successful. They will work like a servant to gain favor and position. This attitude seeks **self-promotion** and not **Godly promotion.**

These "so called" servants will try to serve, act like it's all about you, but, let me warn you…they are out to use you.

They use the servant role as a ploy, a mask to get them where they really don't belong. They will have outbursts of sarcasm. They will act like they are going to follow instructions but in reality they are rebellious. Their substance will leak through the false image. There is no real servant in them. They do the work of a servant to gain access to someone or something. Their focus is to be noticed and not to serve. My mentorship is "try" before you trust. Qualify before you open access to your favor. They are using you!

What is the problem? They do possess a heart of a servant. They have the actions of a servant but not the motive. They are hiding in your midst right now, wearing the servant cloak but in reality they are a Judas waiting to sell you out for the next level. Don't think they won't. **They will sell you out swiftly and quickly for their own gain.**

Exposing the Judas around you isn't as hard as you think. I can tell you a sure and foolproof plan. Start treating those around you, who say they want to serve you, like a servant and watch and listen. Monitor what they say and how they act. Either they will be excited to serve or they will start to complain, moan and develop an attitude. They may quote their resume and talk about all they have done. Cut these kinds of people loose. I know this sounds hard, but you are actually protecting those who are connected to you for the right reasons. You are being the Godly leader you are called to be. You are doing what is uncomfortable for the whole vision and not just yours. These kinds of people are out to self-promote at the expense of you and your ministry!

IMMEDIATELY FIRE DISLOYALTY

I have a pastor friend who says, **"Immediately fire disloyalty."** I felt like this statement was made with no mercy the first time I heard it. I have since changed my mind because disloyalty is a heart problem. Fire people immediately if you discover this attitude in those who *say* they are helping you build the Kingdom of God or even trying to help you build your business. Trust me; you will thank me later. These people aren't promoting you; they are weighing you down. You are now anchored to an unchangeable pattern. They will create sleepless nights for you. They will cause the atmosphere in your ministry to become weakened. You will spend hours pondering what is wrong or what is missing. The truth is that it's all attached to unfaithful and disloyal connections.

Monitor those who keep asking questions about who is betraying whom.

The night that Jesus was arrested, he made a statement to his disciples, *"One of you will betray me tonight."* The disciples looked around the table and asked,

"Is it I, Lord?" All of them were wondering who it would be. The only one that didn't ask was Judas. John asked, **"Who is it, Lord?"** and Judas said **nothing**. Why?

First, Judas knew he was the one. Second, the others asked if it would be them because they had thought about it or talked about it at one time or another. John asked, *"Which one of them is it Lord?"* John never had one bad thought about Jesus. John never spoke an ill word or thought of betrayal. He was clear in his heart. He knew he would never betray Jesus.

Watch out for those who are too quiet around you when you are looking for support. Silent people are the ones you cannot be sure of, in my opinion. When you are looking for verbal support, the silent kind could very easily be your Judas. Don't take silence as a sign that they are with you. **Question them openly; make those who say nothing respond to you.** They will show their attitude when they speak. Let's look at a servant's heart.

A SERVANT'S HEART

A servant's heart is to serve without looking for anything at all. They will take care of your problems without looking for a hand out or trying to gain your access. They do what they do because they love God and they love you and what you stand for.

I had a Spanish Pastor that came to my church from Miami, Florida years ago. When he first came to our church, he asked me, *"What can I do for this church?"* I responded that we needed someone who would be willing to keep the bathrooms clean.

He never said anything about it, nor did I. One day, I was walking by the restroom when all I heard someone singing and crying out loud in the men's room. I approached the door and heard something absolutely amazing. I peeked in through the door and saw a grown man crying on his hands and knees cleaning the bathroom floor. The whole time he was cleaning he was saying, *"Oh God, thank you for allowing me the opportunity to serve you and clean your house. Lord, I praise you and ask you to bless all those who enter these doors."*

He wasn't our Spanish pastor at that point, nor was he in any leadership or staff position. I was so moved in my heart that I thought to myself, this man is a real servant! This man became our full time Spanish pastor a year later. He is still a servant to this day. I can tell you this, after years of ministry I have only seen a few who I could confidently say are real servants.

God will always find a way to promote real servants. I know that there are ten camels full of good stuff set up for these kinds of people in our churches. I know that there is a harvest for all those who remain a servant in the Body of Christ.

- Ministry isn't about buildings, events or programs.
- Ministry isn't about the size of your congregation.
- Ministry is about **servant-hood**.
- Ministry is about taking care of those who are hurting, who are in need and don't know what to do.
- Ministry is turning to the Lord and asking Him what you can do to change someone's life.

Servant-hood will produce the **faithfulness of God**. Read the whole story about Rebekah and listen to the Holy Spirit. You will be changed, as I was. Serving people is not a weakness; serving people is the very heart of God.

Maybe you are reading this book and you have made the statement, *"I have nothing to sow."* Well, that's not true.

There will never be a day in your life where you won't have something to sow. You will always have time, even if you don't have any money. Make time a seed and sow it. Serve God's house, be a servant and get ready for the Lord to release your camels of good "stuff." Servant-hood will produce the **F.O.G.** (The Faithfulness of God)

Pray this prayer;

Lord, help me to be a servant. Help me to understand that life is not all about me. Help me to put You in the forefront of all I do. Lord, restore to me the joy of my salvation. The real joy of the Lord is to put Jesus first, others second and myself last.

Lord, I ask you to forgive me for all the bad attitudes I have portrayed to my leaders. I pray right now for my pastor and all the leaders in my church. I confess increase and health to their lives. Lord, I will never again talk about someone or do anything for my selfish gain.

In Jesus' Name, Amen!

Chapter 6

Attitude Produces Favor or Failure

"You must have the same <u>attitude</u> that Christ Jesus had.
Philippians 2:5 NLT

Who, being in very nature God, did not consider equality
with God something to be used to his own advantage;
rather, he made himself nothing by taking the very nature
of a servant, being made in human likeness. And being
found in appearance as a man, he humbled himself by
becoming obedient to death- even death on a cross!"
Philippians 2:6-8 NIV

"Therefore, since Christ suffered in his body, arm
yourselves also with the same <u>attitude,</u> because whoever
suffers in the body is done with sin." 1 Peter 4:1 NIV

Attitude is a very important - or maybe I should say a right attitude - if you plan to move up to the next level. The right attitude can create promotion, and the wrong attitude can create your demise. **Favor or Failure** is a choice. The attitude you decide to have will decide favor or failure in your life.

ATTITUDE
1. The position or posture assumed by the body in connection with an action, feeling, mood, etc. 2. A manner of acting, feeling, or thinking that shows 3. One's disposition, opinion, etc 4. One's disposition, opinion, mental set, etc.

Attitude creates Atmosphere. Atmosphere will decide what seeds God will release in your life. Seeds decide your harvest!

Seeds guarantee a future.

The seed you sow leaves your hand, but it doesn't leave your life. It enters your future where it begins to set up your harvest. Your seed enters your future and announces your arrival. Seeds into the Kingdom of God *guarantee a future.* It all hinges on your attitude.

Attitude draws people to you or runs them away.

Your attitude will draw people to you or drive them away from you.

69

"When someone dreads your entry, they've already planned your exit."

Have you ever been around someone who always seems to have a bad attitude? How do you feel when you leave their presence? They can drain your energy. Negative people create negative atmosphere. A negative attitude will rob the atmosphere of faith. Where there is no faith... there is no expectation... there is no hope; miracles become a mere memory of something that happened in the past.

Some people say those who have a bad attitude have a **"chip on their shoulder."** They always have a rotten attitude no matter what happens. No one wants to hang around those who always have a negative attitude.

Attitudes will open doors or close them. The difference between a bad attitude and a good attitude is you. A good attitude is a decision, not a feeling. You can't feel your way into a great attitude; you have to make up your mind every day to have one. Your attitude will open the doors of access or close them.

CHANGE IS THE DOOR TO AN ATTITUDE ADJUSTMENT.

You must be willing to change if you want to have a great attitude. No one is born or has the gift of a great attitude. I'm not convinced that there is a gift called **"attitude."** I believe that attitude is a conscious decision you make in your mind. You must make the necessary effort to raise your thinking in order to have a good attitude.

Make up your mind that you are not going to let bad circumstances influence your attitude. No matter what is happening to you, learn the secret that will propel you out of your present situation. That secret is to **PRAISE GOD, NO**

MATTER WHAT! Praise is the power that brings God into your atmosphere. You will begin to worship when God enters your atmosphere. Worship is the ability to interact with God in such a way that you will start to see things the way God see them.

I begin to get a whole new look at my situation when I climb up to God's level of perspective. There is a surge of **faith!** Faith is reaching out into nowhere and hanging onto nothing until it turns into something.

> **Faith is being able to reach out into nowhere and hang onto nothing until it turns into something.**

The company you keep can also affect your attitude! I don't have to know much about you. All I need to do is see who your close friends are. Your friends will tell me a lot about you. You will always attract like-minded people. Our behavior will be the magnet that draws our friends. So, if you can't figure out why you have negative people hanging around you, you might need to check and see if you're like them. **(Birds of a feather flock together.)**

"To be made new in the <u>attitude</u> of your minds; and to put on the new self, created to be like God in true righteousness and holiness." Ephesians 4:23-24 NIV

This scripture tells us to be made new in the attitude of our minds. The right attitude is a mind thing. Good or bad attitudes start in the mind. Believers should daily renew our minds in the Word of God to create the mind of Christ in us. *("Let this mind be in you, which was also in Christ Jesus." Philippians 2:5 KJV).* The mind of Christ will be our defense against   anything that tries to change our attitude. Attitude is the catalyst that can propel you into a season of success.

There is a person in the Bible that kept his attitude in check no matter what happened to him. That man was Joseph. Joseph's right attitude allowed God and others to discover that he could be trusted and promoted.

"Then God remembered Rachel; he listened to her and enabled her to conceive. She became pregnant and gave birth to a son and said, "God has taken away my disgrace." She named him Joseph, and said, "May the LORD add to me another son." Genesis 30:22-24 NIV

Joseph was a type of Christ because he was going to take away the disgrace of his family. His father, Jacob, loved him dearly and began to show him favor at an early age. Joseph's brothers were jealous of him. Those around you may become jealous when you start walking in favor. His brothers plotted to kill Joseph, but they had a change of mind and sold him into slavery instead.

God won't allow what you're going through to kill you. God has a destiny for you to discover, just as He did for Joseph. The going may get tough but the circumstances will not kill you.

Joseph had a destiny, and that destiny was in Egypt. God allowed the circumstances around Joseph to push him into the direction that He needed Joseph to go. Don't let your guard down when things aren't always what you want them to be. Don't complain and moan about what you're going through. Just raise the level of your faith and walk in a right attitude.

"Meanwhile, the Midianites sold Joseph in Egypt to Potiphar, one of Pharaoh's officials, the captain of the guard." Genesis 37:36 NIV

Joseph was sold to Potiphar, one of Pharaoh's officials. Imagine how Joseph must have felt. God had given him a dream that he was going to be so blessed that even his brothers would recognize him and bow down to his favor. Yet, here he was, sold as a servant to Potiphar.

God had not forgotten Joseph.

"Now Joseph had been taken down to Egypt. Potiphar, an Egyptian who was one of Pharaoh's officials, the captain of the guard, bought him from the Ishmaelites who had taken him there. The LORD was with Joseph so that he prospered, and he lived in the house of his Egyptian master. When his master saw that the LORD was with him and that the LORD gave him success in everything he did, Joseph found favor in his eyes and became his attendant. Potiphar put him in charge of his household, and he entrusted to his care everything he owned. From the time he put him in charge of his household and of all that he owned, the LORD blessed the household of the Egyptian because of Joseph. The blessing of the LORD was on everything Potiphar had, both in the house and in the field. So Potiphar left everything he had in Joseph's care; with Joseph in charge, he did not concern himself with anything except the food he ate..." Genesis 39:1-6 NIV

Focus with me on verses 3 and 4.

"When his master saw that the LORD was with him and that the LORD gave him success in everything he did,

Joseph found favor in his eyes and became his attendant. Potiphar put him in charge of his household, and he entrusted to his care..." Genesis 36:3-4

Joseph was living as a servant. His own family put him in this crisis. He was living in a strange country and living with a family trained to serve other gods. Talk about problems...what a mess!

Joseph had something working for him...**his attitude!** Joseph's attitude was never damaged by his circumstances or by what others had done to him. Not one thing that happened to him could rob him of his internal peace. He had what I call inner faith in God and in himself. He possessed a confidence that said to those around him, *"I can make it no matter what."*

Potiphar noticed it. The Bible says that the master saw that the Lord was with Joseph. Potiphar didn't discover this attribute the first time he saw Joseph. Joseph had to show the master that he was a religious man of integrity and character. The master noticed over the course of time that the Lord was with Joseph and the Lord gave him success in all his transactions. Joseph found favor in the eyes of his master. What promoted Joseph? You might say that it was all God's doing. I would disagree! God had a plan, but Joseph had to submit to the plan by **keeping his attitude in check**. He had to be a man who could perform in the hour of trial, and he did! Joseph found favor or grace in the time of need. His attitude got him promoted. His attitude produced the **F.O.G. (Faithfulness of God.)**

ATTITUDE GIVES CLARITY OF MIND!

Don't make the mistake of thinking that when everything seems to be going well you are in your field of dreams. Sometimes God gives us rest stops along the way. Potiphar's house was a place for Joseph to learn the ways of the Egyptians. It was a rest stop for Joseph to gain strength and understanding of his surroundings. Potiphar's house wasn't God's final destination. God had a bigger picture in mind than Joseph just running Potiphar's affairs. God was after Pharaoh, and He was going to use Joseph to bless the children of Israel.

Your mind will be clear of all the "stuff" you are complaining about when you are walking in a proper attitude. Your mind will be completely alert to what God is doing and the blessings that you do have. Then when the enemy comes to test you, you will be ready to run. This very thing happened to Joseph. The enemy tried to destroy the integrity of Joseph.

"...Now Joseph was well-built and handsome, and after a while his master's wife took notice of Joseph and said, "Come to bed with me!" But he refused..." Genesis 39:6-8 NIV

"...My master has withheld nothing from me except you, because you are his wife. How then could I do such a wicked thing and sin against God?" And though she spoke to Joseph day after day, he refused to go to bed with her or even be with her. One day he went into the house to attend to his duties, and none of the household servants was inside. She caught him by his cloak and said, "Come to bed with me!" But he left his cloak in her hand and ran out of the house. Gen 39:9-12 NIV

Joseph was a good-looking man and Potiphar's wife desired him and set out to have him. She tried time after time to get this man to fall into her trap. Joseph's attitude was set so high that he responded to Potiphar's wife with these words, *"I have been given charge over everything in my master's house, and he has held nothing from me except you his wife. How can I do this against my master?"*

Joseph ran from her grip and left his cloak behind in the process. Joseph was making a statement.

"You can have my cloak, but you can't have my character."

We have the ability to better understand our enemy when our attitude is in check and not focusing on all the bad that's going on around us. Joseph was able to keep his wits about what was going on with Potiphar's wife. He kept enough sense to run in that situation. This woman was wicked. She falsely accused Joseph of attacking her, and her husband believed her. Potiphar's anger burned and he put Joseph into the king's prison.

"When she saw that he had left his cloak in her hand and had run out of the house, she called her household servants. "Look," she said to them, "this Hebrew has been brought to us to make sport of us! He came in here to sleep with me, but I screamed. When he heard me scream for help, he left his cloak beside me and ran out of the house." She kept his cloak beside her until his master came home. Then she told him this story: "That Hebrew slave you brought us came to me to make sport of me. But as soon as I screamed for help, he left his cloak beside me and ran out of the house." When his master heard the story his wife told him, saying, "This is how your slave treated me," he burned with anger. Joseph's master took him and put him in prison, the place where the king's prisoners were confined." Genesis 39:13-20 NIV

Joseph was falsely accused and thrown into prison for something he didn't do. Did Joseph throw up his hands and give up? Did he lie down and say, *"I've had enough?"* Did he sit in his prison cell and cry about how innocent and loyal he had been? Did he have the attitude so many get when nothing seems to go right? Did he boast and say, **"Look at all I've given up and done for the Lord and this is how I am repaid."** No, Joseph made good of a bad situation.

He kept his way of thinking and good disposition, no matter what happened to him. No wonder he was so favored by the Lord. Nothing seemed to move this man into depression; not circumstances, not the enemy and not even being falsely accused. He stayed clear, no matter what, in thought and actions! Real winners never lose.

> *WINNERS never lose!*
> *If they aren't winning, they're learning.*

"But while Joseph was there in the prison, the LORD was with him; he showed him kindness and granted him favor in the eyes of the prison warden. So the warden put Joseph in charge of all those held in the prison, and he was made responsible for all that was done there. The warden paid no attention to anything under Joseph's care, because the LORD was with Joseph and gave him success in whatever he did." Genesis 39:20-23 NIV

Once again, Joseph was not put in charge by the warden right after he arrived in jail. Over the course of time, Joseph showed the warden through his attitude that the Lord was with him, that the Lord showed kindness to him and that he walked in the F.O.G. (favor of God).

What the devil assumed was Joseph's demise actually propelled Joseph into his next season of promotion. Satan always makes the mistake of assuming that what was supposed to kill you, will. Therefore, Satan leaves you for dead. Psalms 118 was written for Joseph and anyone who has been where Joseph was.

"I shall not die but live and declare the works of the **Lord."
Psalms 118:17 KJV**

God always shows his mighty hand when we keep our faith in tact and our attitude in check. God works all things to our good according to His purpose *(Romans 8:28)*.

Joseph unlocked the favor of God once more.

God was ready to orchestrate another level of His plan. He was ready to move the right people into Joseph's life. (**Access!**)

When God wants to bless you, He will schedule the right people to connect to you.

Sometimes, the *wrong place* can become the right place to gain access. What seems to be the wrong place could actually become the only place to find promotion. Many miss their season of promotion because they can't see how God is going to do what He promised in a bad season. Don't allow the season of trouble, pain or problems to block you from the God who is bigger than your situation. Don't let the situation become larger than your revelation. Think about it. You wouldn't perceive that prison would be a place where you could find promotion, but with God all things are possible. Never allow your situation or circumstances to dictate your future. What should have killed you and destroyed you will be what God uses to push you forward to take your place and collect your harvest.

"Pharaoh was angry with his two officials, the chief cupbearer and the chief baker, and put them in custody in the house of the captain of the guard, in the same prison where Joseph was confined. The captain of the guard assigned them to Joseph, and he attended them." Genesis 40:2-4 NIV

Joseph ministers to these men and in return asks them to remember him.

Joseph interprets their dreams- the butler was restored and went back to work in Pharaoh's palace. The butler didn't forget about Joseph. Two years passed and one day the butler saw that the king was upset and perplexed. So the butler remembered Joseph and told the king that there was a man in his prison that could interpret dreams. Pharaoh sent for Joseph.

"So Pharaoh sent for Joseph, and he was quickly brought from the dungeon. When he had shaved and changed his clothes, he came before Pharaoh. Pharaoh said to Joseph, "I had a dream, and no one can interpret it. But I have heard it said of you that when you hear a dream you can interpret it." "I cannot do it," Joseph replied to Pharaoh, "but God will give Pharaoh the answer he desires." Genesis 41:14-16 NIV

"Then Joseph said to Pharaoh, "The dreams of Pharaoh are one and the same. God has revealed to Pharaoh what he is about to do. The seven good cows are seven years, and the seven good heads of grain are seven years; it is one and

the same dream. The seven lean, ugly cows that came up afterward are seven years, and so are the seven worthless heads of grain scorched by the east wind: They are seven years of famine." Genesis 41:25-27 NIV

"Then Pharaoh said to Joseph, "Since God has made all this known to you, there is no one so discerning and wise as you. You shall be in charge of my palace, and all my people are to submit to your orders. Only with respect to the throne will I be greater than you." So Pharaoh said to Joseph, "I hereby put you in charge of the whole land of Egypt." Then Pharaoh took his signet ring from his finger and put it on Joseph's finger. He dressed him in robes of fine linen and put a gold chain around his neck. He had him ride in a chariot as his second-in-command, and people shouted before him, "Make way!" Thus he put him in charge of the whole land of Egypt. Then Pharaoh said to Joseph, "I am Pharaoh, but without your word no one will lift hand or foot in all Egypt." Genesis 41:39-44 NIV

Joseph went from the prison to the palace because of a good attitude and faith in a good God. He had a change of address in just twenty-four hours.

Hang on to your faith and keep your attitude in check. Your attitude will produce the F.O.G. (Faithfulness of God). You are about twenty-four hours from an address change: from poverty to prosperity, from sickness to health, from worry to worship, from death to life, from divorce to a good marriage. Your whole life could change in just twenty-four hours. Just keep the faith and hang on.

Chapter 7

Waiting on Godly Promotion

Will Produce the Faithfulness of God

When we begin to discern how important it is to equip ourselves to protect our atmosphere, then we will limit who enters our atmosphere because they can hinder or promote us. We must protect our environment and interests. I've said this many times. Demons don't destroy ministries, people do! Matter fact demons don't do a lot of things they get blamed for. People destroy people. People kill people. I hate when someone says to me we need to control guns in America. I ask why? They reply, "Because guns kill." I say that's not true. I own many guns. They sit in my gun safe. I've never gone to that safe and caught a gun sitting there asking me to kill someone. No! People who use guns kill. People hurt people. People can help people. It's all in their decisions.

I believe that one of the reasons for church splits and ministry wars is because we allow people with the wrong attitude to help. What should you look for? Look for those with a self-centered attitude. When someone is constantly promoting himself or herself, they have a hidden agenda. Monitor how those people only want to serve when you have someone important or if you are doing something that is important. Maybe you are one of those who thinks that they would never try to **self-promote**, but unfortunately, many people do!

I will never again put a person in a position just to fill a void or to have someone work in an area in which he or she is not completely qualified and gifted to take it all the way to the highest level. When a church is trying to make a mark in the Kingdom of God and has limited finances, limited resources and limited people to choose from, we tend to just let anyone fill a position. When someone comes to us expressing a desire to help, there is a surge of excitement, because we need workers. **Caution:** if we don't qualify them, our excitement will quickly turn into exasperation. Let me give you a great statement.

"IF YOU CAN'T BE CORRECTED, YOU CAN'T BE CONNECTED."

Those who can't be corrected and won't let you correct them have a Jezebel spirit in them. This Jezebel spirit is what causes them to not be able to submit to Godly leadership.

Jezebel is a controlling spirit and that spirit is out to do one thing; destroy the works of a man of God. Jezebel will go around your congregation and work all those who are dissatisfied with your leadership. When you're a leader, there is no way that everyone will at all times be completely for you. Those people who have a rift with their leaders would probably get over their feelings and disgruntled attitude. Then here comes Jezebel, the controlling spirit, to hook up with their hurts and before long convinces them to overthrow the leadership with rebellion. Now the Word of God says that rebellion is a form of witchcraft.

> **If You Can't Be Corrected You Can't Be Connected!**

How do we deal with Jezebel? We destroy that spirit! You can't make peace with this spirit. You will not be able to contain it or control it. Don't think for one moment that you can ignore it and it will disappear. The only course of action is to immediately go after Jezebel and cut her head off!

Destroy it! By the power of the Word of God, raise your sword and strike the head of Jezebel. Dethrone her fast and hard. Make no treaty with this spirit. It will destroy you if you don't destroy it.

Whatever promotes you will have to sustain you. If self is promoting someone other than self, they will have to be the power to sustain him or her. If man is promoting you, then men will have to sustain you. Whatever is promoting you will have to have the power within it to hold you up in hard times and in difficult times. Man will fail you, self will fail you… but God will not! If God is promoting you then it will be God who holds you up and keeps your head above the cloud of despair and anguish.

Those who are seeking leadership for the sole purpose of being promoted to a certain position will never make it. Time is the dynamic and God is the promoter. If the person looking for leadership isn't willing to wait for the proper time, they will become your problem. So watch those who complain about how long it is taking for them to receive their promotion. Guard yourself from people who are only interested in a position or promotion. When you find those who are willing to wait on God, they are the ones you want to surround yourself with. When you find a person who only talks about when, where and why they haven't been used or ask why others are being used more than them…those are the very ones who are self-promoting. They are the Judases that will betray you for their own selfish promotion.

Men or women who are willing to wait on Godly promotion, no matter how long it takes, will find the **F.O.G. (Faithfulness of God).**

One of the greatest examples in the Word of God of a man who showed the qualifications for leadership is Joshua.

"Then Moses set out with Joshua his aide, and Moses went up on the mountain of God." Exodus 24:13 NIV

"So the LORD said to Moses, "Take Joshua son of Nun, a man in whom is the spirit of leadership, and lay your hand on him. Have him stand before Eleazar the priest and the entire assembly and commission him in their presence. Give him some of your authority so the whole Israelite community will obey him." Numbers 27:18-20 NIV

Notice that God appointed Joshua to be the predecessor to Moses. God commanded Moses to lay his hands on him and give him a portion of his anointing.

When we are allowing those around us to step up, we must empower them to have some authority. We can only do this if we have confidence in the person we are appointing. If I, as a leader, am not sure that you are out for my best interest and the interest of my church, then I will be hesitant to appoint you in an assistant's role.

What does it really mean to be an assistant? An assistant is really someone who is willing to take up the areas that you as the leader don't have time to do or want to do.

If you study the relationship between Moses and Joshua, you will find the word "aide" popping up often. Joshua was Moses' aide, or assistant. Now Joshua was picked by God and trained by man. God will always have someone mentor you and that someone may not be the one to take you all the way; but, no matter what, you must stay in your assistant role until such a time as God sees fit to promote you.

Assistant is nothing more than a servant to the leader. Webster defines the word assistant as *1. Assisting; helping; that serves as a helper; a person who assists or serves in a subordinate position; helper 2. A thing that aids.*

An assistant is someone who God has seen fit to stand beside the leader without any threat of a hostile takeover. We need to be very cautious as leaders when allowing someone this kind of access. The sin of familiarity can destroy you and your relationship with your assistant.

When we are in need of an assistant, we need to wait on the Lord and allow God the time it takes to pick us a Joshua. What we tend to do as leaders is to move faster than God has planned for us to move. Don't just put people around you who you like or who desire to be around you. Find those who will add to your weakness. Only a fool believes he has no limitations! Build to your weaknesses. Understand what it takes for a team fit. When looking, make sure that the person you are looking for has your best interest in mind.

Seek the Lord and make sure that there is a team fit... that the person you are allowing access has no problem with being asked to leave the room or handle not being told everything. Make certain that the person you are allowing around you has your best interest in mind and not their promotion. A real assistant has no problem with being second, until such time as God promotes him to be number one.

When God was getting ready to give Moses the law, He had Moses go up to Mount Horeb... the mountain of God. God informs Moses to come to the mountain alone and to make sure no one sees him coming.

A good assistant has to be able to let you go alone sometimes, but in your absence, he is to stay focused on what you have put into the people. There are always two kinds of leaders in your camp. First, there are the Aarons who are only listening to what the people want. Second, there are the Joshuas who, no matter what the people want, stay loyal to you.

Aaron is one of those leaders who is always lending an ear to the complaints of the crowd. This is dangerous, because when you are gone and not in front of the crowd, your leaders must stand in your place with the same convictions, as you would have. Aaron leaders are the ones who listen and then reply to the crowd and give them what they want. What happens in this scenario is the one who is giving the people what they are demanding instead of following you and your instruction, undermines you as the main leader. This will bring punishment down upon the people. Watch out for those who are always concerned with what the crowd is complaining about; they may be the very one feeding the crowd the information.

When setting up your assistant, make sure they possess the ability to be a servant. The first criterion for an assistant is servant-hood.

Joshua was one of those assistants willing to wait on Godly promotion. Just think for a moment how long it took Joshua to finally take his place as the leader of the Israelites.

He was one of the spies who entered the land of promise and returned with the report that they could take the land. Others were convinced that the giants were bigger and stronger than God.

He was the one who had to wait for Moses while he was spending time with God on top of the mountain. When Moses returned, Joshua was waiting half way down the mountain.

He had to wander for forty years with the children of Israel and wait while God punished all those who grumbled and complained. Can you imagine what Joshua must have felt when he heard the law of God and that God was going to kill off all those who disobeyed? Talk about being patient! Most of our assistants can't wait five years, let alone forty.

"Because of you the LORD became angry with me also and said, "You shall not enter it, either. But your assistant, Joshua son of Nun, will enter it. Encourage him, because he will lead Israel to inherit it. And the little ones that you said would be taken captive, your children who do not yet know good from bad--they will enter the land. I will give it to them and they will take possession of it. But as for you, turn around and set out toward the desert along the route to the Red Sea." Deuteronomy 1:37-40 NIV

Joshua was not about to take his place any time sooner than when God desired him to do so. Joshua's time finally came.

"Now Joshua son of Nun was filled with the spirit of wisdom because Moses had laid his hands on him. So the Israelites listened to him and did what the LORD had commanded Moses." Deuteronomy 34:9 NIV

"After the death of Moses the servant of the LORD, the LORD said to Joshua son of Nun, Moses' aide: "Moses my servant is dead. Now then, you and all these people, get ready to cross the Jordan River into the land I am about to give to them-to the Israelites. I will give you every place where you set your foot, as I promised Moses. Your territory will extend from the desert to Lebanon, and from the great river, the Euphrates-all the Hittite country-to the Mediterranean Sea in the west. No one will be able to stand against you all the days of your life. As I was with Moses, so I will be with you; I will never leave you nor forsake you." Joshua 1:1-5 NIV

When it was Joshua's turn to lead, God was with him every step of the way. He had such power and abilities. He did more than Moses did because God was with him and because Moses mentored him.

There is another person who waited on God and, because of his ability to wait, God was also with him in a mighty way. His name was David.

The power to wait is the power to achieve with less stress. Patience is not something we do well as humans. We are not the kind of people who know how to wait on things. There is power in waiting.

"Yet the LORD longs to be gracious to you; therefore he will rise to show you compassion. For the LORD is a God of justice. Blessed are all who wait for him." Isaiah 30:18 NIV

"Hast thou not known? hast thou not heard, that the everlasting God, the LORD, the Creator of the ends of the earth, fainteth not, neither is weary? there is no searching of his understanding. He giveth power to the faint; and to them that have no might he increaseth strength. Even the youths shall faint and be weary, and the young men shall utterly fall: But they that wait upon the LORD shall renew their strength; they shall mount up with wings as eagles; they shall run, and not be weary; and they shall walk, and not faint." Isaiah 40:28-31 KJV

Joshua was willing to wait and David was willing to wait for Godly timing. Patience is the ability to wait without complaint. Webster has a great definition…

1) The state, quality, or fact of being patient; specif., *a)* the will or ability to wait or endure without complaint *b)* steadiness, endurance, or perseverance in the performance of a task

2) [Chiefly Brit., etc.] SOLITAIRE (sense 3)

Don't you just love this definition! Patience is the product of endurance; the ability to stand in the middle of your life and not allow things to upset you in such a way that you begin to complain about them.

I love the word *"stoicism":* endurance without flinching to pain or pleasure.

When we train ourselves to walk at such a level to be able to wait on Godly promotion, we begin to walk in such power and peace that it will drive the enemy crazy. The key to not failing and missing your destiny is to just keep on walking, no matter what is happening to you. When men are praising you, keep on walking…when they are talking bad about you, just keep on walking…when you are in the storm, just keep on walking.

The storm doesn't have to be moving for you to get out of it sooner. Just keep walking and you will exit your storm sooner than those who decide to sit and complain about it.

PATIENCE IS WAITING WITHOUT COMPLAINING

Patience is waiting on God without complaint. There is no possible way you can praise God at the same time you are complaining about things. With society being so self-satisfying, it's no wonder we don't hear many testimonies about how God brought people out of their crises. When we want something we can't afford, we go to **"rent-a-center."** When we are sick, we immediately grab a bottle of pills instead of the Word of God. We have become a generation who can't wait on anything. We are the **"microwave generation."**

Talk about **revival...renewal...restoration... redemption**. What the kingdom of God needs today is a revival, renewal and restoration on the ability to wait on God.

People who cannot wait will never be the ones who will build the church. They will always be the ones who bounce from ministry to ministry. They will never be satisfied and never plant themselves in one place long enough to ever experience a harvest. We as leaders need to seek the Holy Spirit for wisdom and discernment so we can discover these impatient people before they destroy all the work that we've done. What has taken us years to build, they will destroy in months.

Three times God handed King Saul over to David. David would not take the throne for himself or by his own hand. David would not touch God's anointed, no matter what the circumstance. David's attitude was one of character and integrity. If God wants me to be king, then God himself will have to make it happen. No wonder he was a man after God's own heart. He was willing to wait, no matter how long it took for God to promote him.

Waiting on Godly promotion will produce the FOG. (**Faithfulness of God**)

So if you've been in an area of ministry for quite some time and you're beginning to feel the strain of your service, don't complain; just raise your hands and praise the Lord. God exalts and God puts down. If you're supposed to be promoted, God will open the door for you and **God will be faithful!**

Debt is the proof of being impatient.

Chapter 8

Faith Applied Will Produce the Faithfulness of God

Satan's information is always free!

God's is never free. It will cost you something...

Anything worth having has a price tag attached to it.

Faith is God's currency... If you desire anything from the Word of God to be applied to your life - healing, prosperity, victory, salvation, health and a relationship with God - you must cash in the currency of faith!

Faith is God's economics released. Faith is God's power applied to your belief system. Faith is the source that will take you into new territory without worry and fear. Faith will cause something to rise in you that will give you all the internal substance you need to face the giants of life, the lions of anger and the fire of temptation. Faith is what the whole basis of Heaven is built upon. You will never advance to the level of great and uncommon achievements if you can't walk in faith.

> **Satan's information is free- God's will cost you!**

You must first conquer fear if you want to walk in faith

Fear is the proof faith has entered your season.

The first thing people usually feel when they decide to exercise their faith is fear; especially when you are willing to take a chance and step out into unfamiliar places. Everyone who makes movement and decides to leave their comfort zone will have a surge of fear. Fear is our built-in warning system that says to us *"this may fail"* and cause us to ask ourselves what's next if it does. We turn our warning

95

system into a power that controls when fear becomes the driving force in us. Anything that controls us becomes what we worship and respect. Fear is in control when we stop making advancement. *Fear is a paralyzing power...* fear can be intimidating and cause you to become so worried that you won't be able to do anything but sit in a room and settle for mediocrity. Satan will assign a **spirit of fear** to you when he wants to stop what you are doing. That demon's job description is to destroy any hope of victory and make your life a living prison of **fear, worry, stress and anxiety.**

Fear will cause you to become ineffective and powerless. Fear will stop you from giving, stop you from praising and stop you from witnessing. Fear is one spirit you had better not take sitting down.

Fear was the very reason the children of Israel didn't enter the Promised Land the first time and wandered in it for forty years. Fear will cause you to look at your situation and not at what God has promised.

"But the men that went up with him said, we be not able to go up against the people; for they are stronger than we. And they brought up an evil report of the land which they had searched unto the children of Israel, saying, The land, through which we have gone to search it, is a land that eateth up the inhabitants thereof; and all the people that we saw in it are men of a great stature. And there we saw the giants, the sons of Anak, which come of the giants: and we were in our own sight as grasshoppers, and so we were in their sight." Numbers 13:31-33 KJV

What stopped them from advancing forward? It wasn't the giants they were facing; the children of Israel failed to advance to the next level because of their mentality. They couldn't make the jump from desert living. Their views of themselves were more damaging than the enemy itself.

They couldn't shake the welfare mentality. God fed them, clothed them and protected them as long as they were in the desert. They didn't want to do anything but wander around and let something or someone else take care of them. God doesn't want lazy children. He wants those who are willing to work and fight for what they want. Trust God all the way? Yes! Sit down, do nothing and wait for God to do everything? NO! That is welfare.

They said, *"We are in our own sight as grasshoppers."*

Remember, it is God who got you this far, and it will be God who will carry you the rest of the way even when you encounter problems.

I've come too far to fail… I've come too far to quit… I've come too far to allow the spirit of fear to stop me.

We must create a picture in our minds that we are bigger than the problem, because God has sent us. Greater is He that is in us, than he that is in the world. We are possessing because we are **possessed. God possesses us!**

Fear lives in the crevices of the mind...
Fear will stop the faithfulness of God.

We must understand that *faith is God's currency* and that *fear is Satan's currency*. You will have to cash in the currency of faith if you desire anything from Heaven. You have to spend your faith if you want to produce a miracle. Faith is the door that holds all of the blessings of God. Faith is the key that unlocks that door, and fear is the key that allows hell the power it needs to keep the door from opening. We must get this thought. The love of God is different than the blessings of God. I did nothing to initiate the love of

God. He loves us unconditionally. However, the blessings of God are activated through faith. We must initiate our faith if we are going to walk in the blessings.

FEAR WAS THE REASON FOR JOB'S ATTACK

Job 3:25 shows us that Job's fear opened the door for his season of loss. *"What I feared has come upon me; what I dreaded has happened to me." (NIV)*

The enemy knew what to do to Job. Job gave his adversary the key He needed to attack him. Let me be clear. God didn't put that fear in Job.

Fear does not come from God. God has not given us a spirit of fear.

"For God hath not given us the spirit of fear; but of power, and of love, and of a sound mind." 2 Timothy 1:7 KJV

God gave us the spirit of power, and of love and a sound mind. You will have a mind that is full of peace when you are walking in faith. The word of God says there is perfect peace for those whose mind is set on Jesus (Isaiah 26:3). God gives us perfect peace when we are focusing on Him and not our problems. You must walk in love in order to walk in power. Real love produces Godly power.

"...God is love. Whoever lives in love lives in God, and God in them. This is how love is made complete among us so that we will have confidence on the day of judgment: In this world we are like Jesus. There is no fear in love. But perfect love drives out fear, because fear has to do with punishment. The one who fears is not made perfect in love." 1 John 4:16-18 NIV

I like the acronym I heard about fear:

F.   False
E.   Evidences
A.   Appearing
R.   Real

Let's bind together right now and defeat the spirit of fear! I agree with you and by the power of the Word of God that we draw the sword of faith and cut off the head of the spirit of fear. In the name of Jesus, we will not walk or live in the prison of fear another day. God has not given me fear. I am a child of God and have been given the power to destroy all the powers of the devil. I am free from fear today.

In the name of Jesus, AMEN! It is done!

This chapter was titled "faith applied." Faith alone will not produce results. Every person has been given a measure of faith.

"…in accordance with the faith God has distributed to each of you." Romans 12:3 NIV

"For I say, through the grace given unto me, to every man that is among you, not to think of himself more highly than he ought to think; but to think soberly, according as God hath dealt to every man the measure of faith." Romans 12:3 KJV

God has dealt to every person a measure of faith. Faith is not something we are unfamiliar with. We operate in natural faith every day. Do you sit in your car and wonder if it will start? No, you just turn that key with the assurance that your car will start. You had faith in the manufacturer to create a vehicle that will start.

Do you thoroughly check a chair to make sure it can hold you before sitting down? No, you just sit down. That takes a measure of faith. You believed that the chair will hold you.

If you are driving down the road and are about to go under a bridge, do you pull over and make sure the bridge is going to stand while you're underneath it? Absurd! You don't even give it one thought; you just drive right on through without a minute of worry. Bridges fall all over the world, but you showed faith in the engineer, in the contractor and in the concrete. You applied your belief system and went right on forward without hesitation.

Yet, when it comes to healing, prosperity, or protection we have this inner worry that we might be missing it. We start to make up our own theology about what God meant. We rewrite our theology to accommodate our tragedies. Faith applied will produce the **faithfulness of God.** The power of Heaven is to believe. Jesus said that all things are possible to him that believes. Nothing is impossible for God. God asked Jeremiah a question that fits right now... *"Is there anything too hard for God?"* NO! (Jeremiah 32:27)

Just believe...faith applied and not just faith. It must be applied. You must first build the measure of faith you have so that you can apply it.

Faith comes by hearing

But what does it say? "The word is near you; it is in your mouth and in your heart," that is, the message concerning faith that we are proclaim: If you declare with your mouth, "Jesus is Lord," and believe in your heart that God raised him from the dead, you will be saved. For it is with your heart that you believe and are justified, and it is with your mouth that you profess your faith and are saved. As Scripture says, "Anyone who believes in him will never be put to shame." Romans 10:8-11 NIV

"How, then, can they call on the one they have not believed in? And how can they believe in the one of whom they have not heard? And how can they hear without someone preaching to them? And how can anyone preach unless they are sent? As it is written, "How beautiful are the feet of those who bring good news!" But not all the Israelites accepted the good news. For Isaiah says, "Lord, who has believed our message?" Consequently, <u>faith comes from hearing the message,</u> and the message is heard through the word of Christ." Romans 10:14-17 NIV

Faith comes through hearing the Word of God. How can you hear the Word? You have to speak what you believe out of your mouth. Confession is the key to applying your faith. Now hold it. Are you thinking that you can confess a new car and a new house? **You're right; you can, ON ONE CONDITION!** That condition is that you line up with the Word of God and live according to everything the Word of God says:

- **You're faithful in your tithe.**
- **You're faithful in your giving.**
- **You're faithful in your church attendance**.
- **You harbor no ill feelings toward your Christian brothers and sisters in the Lord.**
- **You hold your tongue and don't talk about people.**

"Now I say, That the heir, as long as he is a child, differeth nothing from a servant, though he be lord of all; But is under tutors and governors until the time appointed of the father. Even so we, when we were children, were in bondage under the elements of the world: But when the fullness of the time was come..." Galatians 4:1-4 KJV

Faith applied will produce... not just faith alone. The level of your understanding will determine the power of your ability to apply your faith.

We will not receive the rights of an heir to claim all that God has promised as long as we continue our walk as children. We will only receive what God believes we can handle.

We can possess enough understanding of faith to be saved but not enough to walk in healing. Our understanding of the Word of God is the key to everything God has set up for us through our maturity as believers. *"...as long as the heir is a child, he is no different than a slave, although he owns the whole estate, he is subject to guardians and trustees..."* You will remain in bondage and under the elements of the world as long as you remain a child.

The church is full of saved, Heaven bound, immature children who do not want to learn anything beyond salvation. Why? Because where much is given, much is required. If you have been at the same spiritual level for some time, be honest with yourself. Aren't you tired of being tossed around by the enemy? Aren't you tired and fed up with having enough of God to save you from...but not enough of God to take you into?

What good is coming out of struggle and bondage only to wander like the children of Israel for forty years in the desert and never enter your next season of promotion?

- In Egypt there was not enough.
- In the wilderness there was just enough.
- In Canaan there was **MORE THAN ENOUGH!**

Faith applied is the ability to believe and the power giving action to what God says, so that you can come out of whatever you are in and move forward into the promise He has given you!

Say this aloud...

"WHEN I COME OUT OF MY MESS. I WILL NOT LEAVE IT EMPTY HANDED. I AM LIVING IN THE OVERFLOW. MY FAITH IS STANDING STRONG TO RECEIVE MY HARVEST. I HAVE APPLIED MY FAITH. I AM BLESSED, HEALED AND DELIVERED FROM ALL BONDAGE AND SLAVERY! I AM FREE. I AM HEALED. I WALK IN POWER AND MIGHT. MY MIRACLE IS RIGHT AROUND THE NEXT TURN. MY GOD HAS NEVER FAILED ME AND I AM NOT GOING TO FAIL EITHER. GLORY TO GOD!"

We must apply our faith... we must use it daily. Faith unused becomes weak.

Read these next passages carefully...

"But someone will say, "You have faith; I have deeds." Show me your faith without <u>deeds,</u> and I will show you my faith by my deeds. You believe that there is one God. Good! Even the demons believe that--and shudder. You foolish person, do you want evidence that <u>faith without deeds is useless</u>? Was not our ancestor Abraham considered righteous for what <u>he did</u> when he offered his son Isaac on

the altar? You see that his <u>faith and his actions were</u> <u>working together, and his faith was made complete by what</u> <u>he did.</u> And the scripture was fulfilled that says, "Abraham believed God, and it was credited to him as righteousness," and he was called God's friend. You see that a person is considered righteous by what they do and not by faith alone. In the same way, was not even Rahab the prostitute considered righteous for what she did when she gave lodging to the spies and sent them off in a different direction? As the body without the spirit is dead, <u>so faith</u> <u>without deeds is dead.</u>" James 2:18-26 NIV

Notice how many times we see the word faith mixed with the word deeds. Don't misinterpret this passage. Works alone will not save you. Works alone will not move Heaven. You must mix your faith with your works. You must believe, and then act on what you believe. Remember, *"Faith comes by hearing the Word of God."* Actions come by believing what you heard.

Faith applied will produce the **faithfulness of God**. God is only going to move at the level of your faith released. Quit blaming God for things you haven't received. It's not God keeping them from you, **it's you!** God already gave you His instructions in Galatians chapter 4; if you remain as a child then you will be no different from a slave. You will be in bondage to the elements of this world.

"When I was a child, I talked like a child, I thought like a child, I reasoned like a child. When I became a man, I put the ways of childhood behind me. For now we see only a reflection as in a mirror; then we shall see face to face. Now I know in part; then I shall know fully, even as I am fully known." 1 Corinthians 13:11-12 NIV

Mature faith will take you to a place where you are able to see and understand fully what the purpose of God is.

"We give thanks to God always for you all, making mention of you in our prayers: Remembering without ceasing your <u>work of faith,</u> and labour of love, and patience of hope in our Lord Jesus Christ, in the sight of God and our Father; Knowing, brethren beloved, your election of God". 1 Thessalonians 1:2-4 KJV

This verse confirms faith applied in three words. Remembering without ceasing your **work of faith**... Faith is work! Whoever said faith was easy was in error. Faith is work. Faith must be applied in order to accomplish what God intended. Appling your faith is work. A better way to say this is - work your faith because faith works.

- When things begin to start happening...**work your faith**!
- When the enemy starts harassing...**work your faith**!
- When depression tries to set in...**work your faith**!
- When hell is all round you and nothing seems to be working...**work your faith!**

Faith will work...when you work it! Faith applied will set you up for a miracle every day of your life. Work your faith, **because faith works.**

Here is a side note for thought that is controversial. Sometimes, God does not remove the problem, no matter how much faith you have.

God allows us to go through sufferings so that we can mature into believers who aren't moved and stirred by what's going on around us. You will possess the faith that gets you through anything when things happening around you can't break your focus.

Real faith is when you're "smack-dab" in the middle of the biggest crisis of your life and somehow you can still offer up praise and worship without any fear or worries about your present situation. God doesn't always want to move the mountain, but He always wants to help us climb it. Here is the power of faith…to hang on and allow God time to get into the pit with you. Think for a moment…if God were always bailing us out, then we would never learn how to be patient.

"Therefore, since we have been justified through faith, we have peace with God through our Lord Jesus Christ, through whom we have gained access by faith into this grace in which we now stand. And we boast in the hope of the glory of God. Not only so, but we also glory in our sufferings, because we know that suffering produces perseverance; perseverance, character; and character, hope. And hope does not put us to shame, because God's love has been poured out into our hearts through the Holy Spirit, who has been given to us. You see, at just the right time, when we were still powerless, Christ died for the ungodly. Very rarely will anyone die for a righteous person, though for a good person someone might possibly dare to die. But God demonstrates his own love for us in this: While we were still sinners, Christ died for us." Romans 5:1-8 NIV

Our trials set us up to learn how to be mature in our walk with God. We frustrate the devil when the devil can't frustrate us through trials and tribulations. When all his efforts seem to do nothing except cause us to praise harder, then pray harder and worship harder.

106

We must be willing to know Jesus in His sufferings if we want the power. The word of God says that if we know Him in His sufferings we will share in His power of resurrection. We, through faith, can walk in the power of Jesus' resurrection. We have RESURRECTION POWER!

FAITH APPLIED WILL PRODUCE THE F.O.G.!

Chapter 9

Giving Will Produce the Faithfulness of God

I have yet to figure out what it is about the prosperity message that gets people so riled up. It doesn't matter how energized a service is when I start talking about money or giving, the whole atmosphere becomes heavy with despair and faces go from smiles to frowns and joy to anger.

PROSPERITY REQUIRES ACCOUNTABLITY

Many people do not want to hear about giving, increase or harvest because prosperity is attached to something you are able to release. A farmer must be first responsible to sow seeds if he wants to reap a harvest. I believe the people do not want to become **accountable** for what they hear. It is one thing to be saved and on your way to Heaven without the knowledge that you can have more, do more and be more. You can bring Heaven's resources into your life. That should make the promise in you jump, but it seems to aggravate most people.

MORE IS GODLY:

My good friend, Dr. Todd Coontz, and I were having a conversation about the prosperity teaching. He said something that shot through my spirit. He said, "**More** is Godly."

You want to know something? That is the truth. Everything in your life should increase when God enters your life. The proof of God is change. Someone once said if you stay in poverty once you've received Jesus in your life it is a disgrace to the Kingdom of God. I know that seems a bit extreme. However, just because it bothers us doesn't make it less true. God expects us to change. He gave us the power, through His Son Jesus, to be able to walk out of our present season into a blessed season. Why would anyone want to stay broke? Why would anyone want to buy into a gospel of Heaven but never believe in a God who wants them wealthy on the earth?

Of course, not everyone will be wealthy. That doesn't mean they couldn't be.   It means they are unwilling to do what it takes to be wealthy. The wealthy do what the un-wealthy are not willing to do.

YOU WILL NEVER BE BROKE ANOTHER DAY IN YOUR LIFE

I will never live a life of poverty! You and I will never experience lack again as long as we obey God's prosperity laws. God has set us up to prosper. Just because people don't want it doesn't mean it's not there. Many in this world don't possess gold but that doesn't mean there's no gold for them to possess. We have to change our thinking. We need to change our conversations. We must stop talking so much about our lack, our losses and our crisis and start speaking about our increase, our blessings and our solutions. I am living in the overflow… how about you?

3 KEYS TO NO MORE LACK

1. Make God your total **source** of supply.
2. Believe you have been anointed for increase.
3. If God can't get it from your hand, He will not place it in your hand.

God has to become your Source. God created us in His image and likeness. In Genesis, you will see God's plan.

God says to the water, "Water, create the fish and all the sea creatures."

Then He told the land to create all the creepy crawly things and the beast of the field. After that, God said, "Let us make man in our image and in our likeness." Water made the fish, land made the beast and God made us. Water is the fish's source. Land is the beast of the field's source and God is our source. Do you see it?

What happens when you take fish out of water and place them on land? They struggle and die. You have moved them from their source and placed them in resource. If you took animals made to live on land and placed them in water, what would happen? They would swim until they couldn't, then they would die. Land is their source, not water. Struggle and death is the proof of resource living.

Man was placed in a garden in the presence of God. God is our Source. As long as man remained in that garden, they lived a life of abundance and blessing. However, we all know the story. Man did not stay. We chose knowledge over presence. So what happened? We were told to leave the garden. Man moved into the *"omnipresence"* of God instead of His concentrated presence.

We were not made to live that way. When we are not living in the Presence of God, we are living on resource instead of God, our Source. Make God your total source of supply.

> You Can Sow Your Seed To Reap A Harvest, Or Eat Your Seed And Choose To Fertilize Someone Else's Harvest

You must believe that you've been anointed by God to live in the overflow. David said in Psalms 23, *"The Lord is my shepherd, I shall not want."* Want is translated from the word lack. When we make God the Source that leads us, we will never walk in lack. David said, ***"My cup runs over."*** He was living in the overflow. We are anointed for overflow. Believe it right now!

Opposition shows up when you talk about the third part of wealth principle. If God can't get it from your hand, He's not going to place it in your hand. That simply means that if I do not sow it, I cannot reap it.

IT"S TIME TO GIVE!

Hell shows up when we teach people that the law of increase and harvest only exists in the power of sowing. Why? Because we become accountable to that principle. If we do not have a harvest, it is because we've refused to sow our seed. You can either sow your seed and reap a harvest, or eat your seed and choose to fertilize someone else's harvest.

INCREASE VERSUS HARVEST!

I was in my sanctuary one day thanking God for giving me what I thought was my harvest after I had sowed a faith seed. My wife and I sow seeds every week. We believe that instead of praying about our financial situation we can activate Luke 6:38… *"Give, and it will be given back to you."*

God changed our financial lives through the power of seed sowing. We have experienced so much increase and blessings that I do not have the time to testify about them all in this book.

Some of My Testimonies:
- *We sowed a faith seed for a car. God had a businessman buy us a C 280 Mercedes.*
- *We bought a 3,000 square foot home that had five bedrooms, three full size bathrooms, 2 fireplaces, an office and a garage. We didn't have to make a*

payment out of our pocket for twelve months because people sowed house payments into our lives.

- *Dr. Mike Murdock took my wife and I to the Holy Land completely paid for.*
- *I had a $6,700.00 debt hanging over my head and someone completely paid off my debt... after I had let go of a $1,250.00 seed.*
- *I sowed a $200.00 seed for a Harley Davidson Motorcycle, and in six months, a friend of mine was led by God to send me a check to pay cash for a Heritage Soft Tail.*

One day, I was thanking God for all His harvests. He spoke back to my spirit these words. ***"That's not your harvest. Those are only increases of my favor."*** I was floored.

Another time, I was driving the "Blue Ridge Parkway" in the mountains of North Carolina on that Heritage Motorcycle that God had given me after I had sowed my seed. I was listening to a praise song, "How Great is Our God." I was looking at my blessing and rubbing the gas tank with tears in my eyes. I said, "God, You've been so good to me."

This is what I heard. ***"Son, I've not even started being good. All you're experiencing is a season of increase... get ready; harvest is on the way."***

GET READY! THIS IS ONLY INCREASE...WAIT UNTIL YOUR HARVEST SHOWS UP!

Get ready for your harvest to show up! Don't let religion and "stinking thinking" rob you of what's rightfully yours by spiritual birth. If you are not already paying your tithe and sowing seeds, start now. Never enter your church service without a seed to sow. I teach my people at the Favor

Center Church to never enter the presence of God empty handed.

Everybody is getting excited about increase…but what about harvest? I was walking around my yard one day praising God for increase and all the things He has done for me. All of a sudden, I felt a quickening in my spirit. The Lord spoke to my heart and said, "You're getting excited about your increase…increase is not your harvest."

If you sow a $100.00 and receive a $1,000.00, that is your increase and not your harvest. Harvest is much greater than increase. Increase is when we gain enough to feel relief for the moment. Harvest is so much bigger.

When Harvest comes, you must be able to eat from it, sow from it, save from it, and take care of the needy from it. I am expecting harvest to come! My harvest and your harvest is a result of our giving. Whatever the enemy tries to do to you, don't let him stop you from planting your seed.

Giving will produce the **F.O.G. (Faithfulness of God)**

"Now there was a famine in the land--besides the previous famine in Abraham's time--and Isaac went to Abimelech king of the Philistines in Gerar. The LORD appeared to Isaac and said, "Do not go down to Egypt; live in the land where I tell you to live. Stay in this land for a while, and I will be with you and will bless you. For to you and your descendants I will give all these lands and will confirm the oath I swore to your father Abraham. I will make your descendants as numerous as the stars in the sky and will give them all these lands, and through your offspring all nations on earth will be blessed, because Abraham obeyed me and did everything I required of him, keeping my commands, my decrees and my instructions." So Isaac stayed in Gerar." Genesis 26:1-6 NIV

"Isaac planted crops in that land and the same year reaped a hundredfold, because the LORD blessed him. The man became rich, and his wealth continued to grow until he became very wealthy. He had so many flocks and herds and servants that the Philistines envied him." Genesis 26:12-14 NIV

Notice that Isaac planted while there was a double famine in the land, and in that same year he reaped a hundredfold because the Lord blessed him. I like this; the man became rich, and his wealth continued to grow until he became VERY WEALTHY!

Riches are what you have; wealthy is who you are.

Don't Love Things More Than People

Harvest is what the church needs to be seeking. Even Jesus said to pray to the Lord of the **harvest** Why? Because so many will be blessed when you reap your harvest. Giving with expectation for a **harvest** makes your focus about others and not about things. Increase is good, but harvest is better. Increase is just enough to lift a financial burden. Increase is for a moment. Harvest last for a season.

LAW OF THE HARVEST

Seed is the power of harvest. We must let go of what is in our hands to be a seed sower. We activate the release of harvest when we release our seed. Remember, there is nothing we have that God didn't really give to us. The truth is if God wanted to, He could just take what He wants from us. He's asking us to be givers so that we won't let what we have own us.

God doesn't care how much you have as long as what you have doesn't have you. People who love things usually use people to get them. When we love people more than things, we will use things to get people. God wants us to love people and use things. Instead, we love things and use people.

One of the major reasons we are not seeing a lot of increase in the church is because we can't handle increase when it happens! I've witnessed this so many times in my church. Someone will ask me to pray for them to get a job. As soon as the Lord answers their prayer, and they get a job, I stop seeing them in church.

So I ask, "Hey where have you been?" Their answer usually goes something like this; "Pastor, man, I'm working so much that I don't have time to be at church." So here's the truth, as soon as you experienced increase you stop pursuing the very Person that gave you the increase. Most of the time, the next season in their lives will be right back where they started. They couldn't handle the blessing.

GOD WILL SUPPLY ALL YOUR NEEDS

Philippians 4:19 says that, *"God will supply all of your needs according to His riches..."* God is a God of provision. God wants to supply you at your level of need. The word need in this passage means land, possessions and money. God wants you to have land, money and possessions. He wants to supply these things to you, not at your financial level, but at His.

It says *"according to His riches..."* The word "riches" in the Greek means "at the level of the Kingdom's wealth." God wants to meet our needs at His level of wealth, not ours. He wants to supply our needs, house, land, money or possessions at His standard and not ours. We're living in the overflow!

The Kingdom of God is about being supplied for. We are not in it to survive; we are in it to thrive. The first miracle and last miracle of *Elijah* was about provision. The first and last miracle of **Elisha** was provisional. Here is the power of prosperity; the first and last miracle of **Jesus** was provisional.

The whole purpose of God sending His son, Jesus, was to provide for us. **God is into our harvest.** He wants us to be blessed so that we can be a blessing. Giving is the key to harvest...sowing is the tool.

Seeds aren't just limited to money; a smile, a kind gesture, a welcomed handshake are all seeds. We are a walking warehouse of seed.

- If you sow love, you will reap love!
- If you sow kindness, you'll reap kindness!
  If you sow mercy, you'll reap mercy!
- **If you SOW MONEY... you're going to REAP MONEY!**

"Give, and it will be given to you. A good measure, pressed down, shaken together and running over, will be poured into your lap. For with the measure you use, it will be measured to you." Luke 6:38 NIV

Notice the word **"IT."** "It" is whatever you sow. Whatever you have given will come back to you, pressed down, shaken together and running over.

The faithfulness of God is hinged on so many aspects of our walk with God. We must learn to understand that there will never be a day in our lives when we can say, **"I have** arrived." We are all in spiritual process, being changed from glory to glory.

Giving is one area that is overlooked in the body of Christ. Satan wants to keep us broke, busted and poor. We will never afford to take the gospel beyond our church walls. We will affect the whole city, state and nation when we become financially liberated.

LEARN TO LET GO AND LET GOD!

When I speak about giving, I don't mean our tithe. Tithe is not seed…tithe is a **payment**. We are commanded by the Lord to pay our tithe. A tithe is 10 percent of what comes to your hand. There seems to be a lot of misunderstanding in the body of Christ about paying tithe. Believers have watered down the responsibility of paying tithe.

Jesus came to change our season! I was living in a season of drought and despair before Jesus entered my life. My whole outlook on life changed when I accepted Him as Lord and Savior. Jesus took me from shallow waters to deep waters. *Would you love to walk out of shallow water living? Do you desire to allow God to change your season and for you to live a life with no more dry seasons?* If you desire to see and experience the **F.O.G. (faithfulness of God)** learn to tithe, sow, and be completely obedient to the Word of God.

We will become blessed when we give what we have to support the Kingdom of God!

In Luke 5, we see exactly what I'm writing about take place.

"And it came to pass, that, as the people pressed upon him to hear the word of God, he stood by the lake of Gennesaret, And saw two ships standing by the lake: but the fishermen were gone out of them, and were washing

their nets. And he entered into one of the ships, which was Simon's, and prayed him that he would thrust out a little from the land. And he sat down, and taught the people out of the ship. Now when he had left speaking, he said unto Simon, Launch out into the deep, and let down your nets for a draught. And Simon answering said unto him, Master, we have toiled all the night, and have taken nothing: nevertheless at thy word I will let down the net. And when they had this done, they inclosed a great multitude of fishes: and their net brake. And they beckoned unto their partners, which were in the other ship, that they should come and help them. And they came, and filled both the ships, so that they began to sink. When Simon Peter saw it, he fell down at Jesus' knees, saying, Depart from me; for I am a sinful man, O Lord. For he was astonished, and all that were with him, at the draught of the fishes, which they had taken" Luke 5:1-9 KJV

The Lord asked Simon to use his ship so that He could teach the people about the Kingdom. Peter had toiled all night fishing, and fishing isn't an easy job. He must have been exhausted. He had worked a physical job all night pulling and casting nets only to come home with no rewards.

What a day this was becoming... after all this work, Jesus was requiring the assistance of his ship and with that assistance came more hours of no sleep. Peter has to sit on the ship and listen to the preaching of the long-winded man of God.

Jesus finished His teaching and looked down at Simon and said, **"Launch out into the deep, and let down your nets for a draught."**

"When He had stopped speaking, He said to Simon (Peter), Put out into the deep (water), and lower your nets for a haul." (The Amplified Version)

The Lord was changing Simon's season from shallow fishing to deep-water fishing. Imagine what was going through the mind of Simon; Jesus was a teacher and He was raised a carpenter and He was instructing Simon on how to fish.

Didn't Jesus realize that Simon had stayed up all night fishing; his nets were already clean and put up for the day, his family was already expecting him to be home? Jesus wants him to go out into deeper waters and lower his nets.

God was about to change his season and change required something on His part.

Watch what Simon said next! *"Master, we have toiled all the night, and have taken nothing: nevertheless at thy word I will let down the net."*

The Amplified Bible says *"…But on the ground of your word, I will lower my nets (again).*

Simon wasn't letting down his net because he wanted to. He wasn't letting down his net because he believed he was going to catch anything. He wasn't even doing it because he had faith and expectation of a blessing. No, Simon said, *"On your word alone am I going to obey."*

He was obeying Jesus' words. His obedience was a clue that He recognized who Jesus was. Obedience is a powerful key for increase. You may have to set aside certain feelings when it comes time to obey. Simon was tired, he was hungry, and he was frustrated. But He wasn't going to miss his opportunity to show Jesus that he would obey even when thought he didn't even feel like it. Simon was saying, "My obedience is not on what I'm feeling, but on what you're saying, Lord!"

When Peter obeyed… **the blessing came**!

"And when they had this done, they inclosed a great multitude of fishes: and their net brake. And they beckoned unto their partners, which were in the other ship, that they should come and help them. And they came, and filled both the ships, so that they began to sink." Luke 5:6-7 KJV

There was so much of a blessing that Simon had to call his partner. Simon calling for his partners is also a powerful thought.

> **AT THE END OF YOUR OBEDIENCE IS GOD'S FAVOR!**

Many had been fishing that night. All found themselves without fish. When Simon obeyed and gave up his time for the gospel to be preached, Simon's blessing was so big that his boat started sinking. Simon called for his partners – not everyone - to come get some of the overflow. Those who are partnering with you are the only ones who are going to qualify for your overflow.

There was so much that the catch almost sank both their ships. Simon gave his ship and his time for the man of God to use. When Jesus was done with Kingdom business, He blessed the **man who gave**! God is faithful to those who learn the power of giving, or sowing seed. One more thing! Peter fell down to his knees, repented and accepted the man of God and was chosen at that time to be one of His disciples. It is only at the end of your obedience that you will discover your miracle.

Favor always follows obedience. Favor comes after you have proven your obedience to God's word. If you divide the word obedience into three parts, the middle word would be "die".

(OBE – **DIE** – ENCE) ---you must be willing to die to your flesh to be a completely obedient believer. The more flesh you kill, the more obedient you will become. Obedience is the qualifier to favor and to God's faithfulness. You must be an obedient giver to be a good giver.

Chapter 10

Conquering Debt Will Produce the Faithfulness of God

You aren't truly free until you are debt free. You cannot be a good giver and not pay your bills.

The worst thing a believer can do is to lag behind on his bills. We all have times of famine and have sown in times of lack, but this shouldn't be the norm. Don't sow what you owe! Sow what belongs to you. Pay your bills first and be faithful to give what you have to the Kingdom of God. I believe that when you get your life in order your finances will begin to turn around. You may start out small but you will finish up **big**!

For example; your power bill is $150.00 and all you have in your checking account is $200.00. Do not sow over what it will cost you to pay your power bill unless you are absolutely sure you have heard from God. God will provide the money to pay your power bill by the due date if He is prompting you to sow at that level of sacrifice.

Be very careful not to let someone stir you up emotionally so that you forget the responsibility to your own commitments. I do not believe that God would impress upon you to sow if it would cost your own reputation to be stained.

Don't misunderstand me; **I'm not saying not to sow**. I'm saying know how and when to sow. Learn to sow continuously, sow often and sow every time you're in an anointed service. Learn to sow at your level and not at the level of others. There would be abundance in our churches if everyone would learn to sow at their level. Unfortunately, in most churches, half of the people sow seeds and the other halves - or more - are freeloaders.

Years ago, my wife and I started learning the principle of prosperity and that the purpose of being blessed is so you can be a blessing. We started sowing weekly seeds in our church. We had a lot of debt at that time so the amount we sowed was a "whopping" $10.00 a week, but that $10.00 was a sacrifice at that season of our lives. Now, we sow over $100.00 a week -or more- above our tithes.

Your seed is never insignificant when it is a sacrifice! *Learn to sow something! If all you have is $1.00, then sow it! It would do more for you in the soil of your faith than in your pocket.*

Money will work for us when we get our finances in order. Money is a tool and tools are supposed to be used. Money was preordained to be used, not worshipped! Money is intended to take care of our needs, not to be slaved over forty to fifty hours a week.

SHOUT RIGHT NOW…"**MONEY COMETH TO MY HOUSE! I WILL GET MY FINANCES IN ORDER.**"

God loves when we make decisions to get our house in order. He is very attentive to our desire to better ourselves and is pleased when we make the necessary efforts to do so. God will get involved with those who desire change. One of the largest setbacks in the body of Christ is **bad credit** and **slow bill payers**. I had a friend who worked in the financing business for many years. He said that many so-called Christians that borrowed money from his company never paid it back or filed bankruptcy. That is disastrous to the reputation of God and us.

Let's change this stigma that is on believers by starting with a heart of repentance. Our character and integrity are on the line. Don't charge something you can't pay cash for now, only to make minimum payments of $10.00 a month, for the next ten to twenty years on a high interest rate. That is illogical. Wait until you have the funds for what you want and learn to trust God.

Debt is a curse and we must break it. The line is drawn here today as you are reading this book and desire to produce the **F.O.G. (Faithfulness of God).** Stop the insanity of debt! Start today; make a budget and stick to it. Start paying off those high percentage credit cards and loans. I assure you that you will see God's participation in your life, finances and family if you start with this. Money will start showing up un-expectantly. God will begin to pour out His power and wisdom in your life when He sees that you desire to become debt free and that He can trust you to bring freedom to others, when you are free.

Let me give you a financial priority list:
1. TITHE
2. SOW
3. BILLS
4. SAVINGS
5. YOURSELF
6. OTHERS
7. RETIREMENT OR INVESTMENTS

You cannot and will not have financial power until you are **debt free**. How can we help others if we are barely getting by? Conquering debt will produce the **F.O.G.**

If you really desire to change your financial future then take the time to study what financial leaders are saying. Go to your local bookstore and inquire about books on budgets, investments, good stewardship and others alike.

We can't change just because we have the desire to; we must take the necessary efforts required to change.

Chapter 11

The Power
Of
PRAISE!

The power of your day is released by the level of your praise! One of the greatest truths believers can learn is to be of good cheer. This is maintaining a spirit of joy and walking in the attitude of praise, even when you're in the center of troubles.

There is a doctrine sweeping through the church that claims we will never have to suffer or go through trials if you can find, gain or learn how to walk in the right kind of faith... **NOT TRUE!**

The truth is that the more understanding of faith you walk in, the more you will be tested for that understanding.

"These things I have spoken unto you, that in me ye might have peace. In the world ye shall have tribulation: but be of good cheer; I have overcome the world." John 16:33 KJV

Jesus tells His disciples "these things" that in me you might have PEACE. In the world, you shall have tribulation. What things?

Shall is an important word. "Shall" states in the text that we will most certainly have trials or tribulations. There is no scripture taken in its context that even hints that we would never suffer. If we plan to live a long life, we had better become confident that we will have to go through heartaches and trials.

The text uses the word tribulation. The Greek meaning to this word is *"pressure, a worn track or rut, and corrosion." As* long as there is breath in your body, you will have to live through some sort of heartaches. Paul said that if you want to know Jesus in the power of His resurrection, you have to be willing to fellowship with Him in his sufferings.

133

"That I may know him, and the power of his resurrection, and the fellowship of his sufferings, being made conformable unto his death." Philippians 3:10 KJV

The good news is that we have a pattern given to us through the Word of God that will propel us through suffering and hardships.

Praise is the power of faith in you. It allows you to lift up your hands in the time of crises, raise your voice in the spirit of boldness and shout that God is able. Praise reminds you that no matter what you are in, God has the ability to get you through it unstained, undamaged and unmoved!

Jesus instructed us to, *"be of good cheer."* The Greek meaning to this phrase means to be bold, courageous and to exercise your courage in times of troubles.

How can we exercise something without an opposite force going against what we are trying to strengthen? You can't! Opposition in life is nothing more than what the weights in a gym are to the physical body. Opposition will cause your faith and praise to develop the spiritual muscles necessary to take you to the next level of promotion and victory. The more you can lift Jesus up in your praise the more you can move mountains with your faith. Praise will bring God into your situation. Praise attracts God to you and where the spirit of the Lord is there is **freedom and victory**.

- What got Paul and Silas through the beating and jail time? *Praise did!*
- What kept Stephen in the book of Acts from seeing his accusers? *Praise did!*
- What allowed David the access necessary to be King? *Praise did!*

David was a man after God's own heart. What did David possess that Saul didn't? David had a spirit of praise in him at all times. He had no problem lifting up his voice and shouting who and what His God could do. David wrote in Psalms 150, *"... let everything that has breath praise the Lord..."*

David stripped down to his undergarments and danced all the way to the top of the mountain where the resting place of the Ark of the Covenant was to be. Praise kept the **F.O.G. (faithfulness of God)** in David's life! Others would have been destroyed for the sin David committed, but God kept his judgment of death away from him because David's heart was always after God.

Think for a moment about the church you attend. Does it have an attitude of Praise and Worship? I'm not talking about singing two songs and sitting down. I'm talking about a spirit and attitude of excitement and expectancy! If your pastor tried to stop it, He couldn't. Praise will develop an attitude of expectancy in the house. Expectancy is the breeding ground for miracles.

We will continue to miss the mark of what God wants for our lives if we don't learn what real worship and praise is all about.

Let me give you an acronym that will help me relate what praise will do for us...**P-R-A-I-S-E**:

P - PUSH BACK THE ENEMY

"Through the praise of children and infants you have established a stronghold against your enemies, to silence the foe and the avenger." Psalms 8:2 NIV

"I will be glad and rejoice in you; I will sing the praises of your name, O Most High. My enemies turn back; they

stumble and perish before you. For you have upheld my right and my cause, sitting enthroned as the righteous judge. You have rebuked the nations and destroyed the wicked; you have blotted out their name forever and ever. Endless ruin has overtaken my enemies, you have uprooted their cities; even the memory of them has perished." Psalms 9:2-6 NIV

Praise is a powerful tool that causes our faith to stay focused on what we know to be true and not on what is going on around us. This knowledge is what the Lord is referring to in the scriptures, *"...and they will know the truth and the truth will set them free..."* (paraphrased). Praise will create an atmosphere around you that will cause whatever is attacking you to back off.

R – RELEASE GOD'S POWER

In Acts 16 Paul and Silas were beaten and thrown into the inner prison and told to be guarded by the chief jailer. Paul and Silas didn't complain or cry out in the confusion of "why" and "how come." They raised their voices in praise and sang unto the Lord a new song -a song of praise- that the whole jail was listening to and so was God. Suddenly, the Spirit of the Lord entered the prison cell. Praise produced and released God's power!

A –ACCESS TO THE PRESENCE OF GOD!

"Therefore, since we have been justified through faith, we have peace with God through our Lord Jesus Christ, through whom we have gained access by faith into this grace in which we now stand. And we boast in the hope of the glory of God. Not only so, but we also glory in our

sufferings, because we know that suffering produces perseverance; perseverance, character; and character, hope. And hope does not put us to shame, because God's love has been poured out into our hearts through the Holy Spirit, who has been given to us. You see, at just the right time, when we were still powerless..." Romans 5:1-6 NIV

Praise gives us access to His presence!

I – INCREASES YOUR CAPACITY TO RECEIVE FROM GOD.

Praise builds your faith! Learn to press in when you feel the anointing of God and shout out your praise. Don't let anyone stop you from praising God. Praise increases your capacity to receive. There were many people who would have never received from the Lord in the Gospel if they didn't cry out their praises to the Lord.

Jesus didn't notice them because of what was troubling them. Jesus noticed them because their praise stood out in a crowd! Their shouts lasted longer than those around them did, and Jesus stopped to notice them because of their praises!

S –SUSTAINING IN TOUGH TIMES!

Praise will hold you up when everything else around you is failing. You can find more strength in praise than in someone trying to help you through your trial.

Praise brings out the joy of the Lord that's in you. The word of God says that there is a greater Source in you than what is in the world. God the Holy Spirit begins to break through the natural realm of understanding when we have an attitude of praise!

Praise will hold you long enough until your miracle can break through.

"Sustain me, my God, according to your promise, and I will live; do not let my hopes be dashed." Psalms 119:116 NIV

"Let me live that I may praise you, and may your laws sustain me." Psalms 119:175 NIV

"Even to your old age and gray hairs I am he, I am he who will sustain you. I have made you and I will carry you; I will sustain you and I will rescue you." Isaiah 46:4 NIV

E –ESTABLISHED AND ENCOURAGED

Praise will establish your identity in the Lord. Praise will set your feet on the rock of revelation when you are facing things that will cause you to question who and what you are all about and your will to build your confidence. That confidence will not exist in what you can do but in what God can do. Praise will establish you faith and encourage you to hang on.

When David was in Ziglag, he lost everything that was dear to him - his wives, his children, his livestock and all his materials.

The word of the Lord tells us what David did to cope with his loss. He encouraged himself in the Lord!

David understood that if he didn't establish within himself that he was of God and that he belonged to God, he would never get back what was stolen. Praise gives us the ability to see things in a different scenery or setting. We will always see things through the eyes of faith and not fear when we learn the art of real worship and praise.

David sought the Lord in what he should do after he encouraged himself in the Lord. David wanted to know if he should pursue the enemy or not, and David wanted to know what he could expect if the instructions from the Lord was to pursue.

God told David to go and pursue the enemy and expect to get it all back. Praise will give us the assurance that no matter what the enemy has stolen, we will get it back when we move forward. Here is the good news...not half or some...we will get it all back!

The right kind of praise will slap the devil in the face. The right kind of praise will bring victory in whatever you're facing and keep you lifted up until God can work on your behalf to make the devil pay!

JUDAH PRAISE

God's answer is interesting to me when the people of God asked Him this question in the Old Testament. *"Who do you want us to send out first?"*

God said, *"Send Judah First."*

"The Israelites went up to Bethel and inquired of God. They said, "Who of us is to go up first to fight against the Benjamites?" The LORD replied, "Judah shall go first." Judges 20:18 NIV

The order of moving with God was as follows: first, the Judah tribe; then the Issachar tribe; and then the Zebulon tribe. Judah means praise. Issachar means honor, and Zebulon means rewards. You can expect honor and reward when you walk in the right praise.

Judah is broken down into three Hebrew words. It is very important to understand the power of three. The Bible says a three-fold cord is not easily broken... *Ecclesiastes 4:12*

The first Hebrew word is **"Yadah"** which means, "to throw up your hands and shout."

"Give thanks (yadah) to the Lord, for his love endures forever." 2 Chronicles 20:21 NIV

"Thus I will bless You while I live; I will (yadah) lift up my hands in Your name." Psalms 63:4 NKJV

"Oh that men would give thanks (yadah) to the Lord for his goodness, and for his wonderful works to the children of men." Psalms 107:15

Other references: Genesis 49:8; 2 Chronicles 7:6; Isaiah 12:4; Jeremiah 33:11

This is the first level of praise. This is where we usher in our Monarch (King). My good friend, Bishop Ceirion Dewar, is from the United Kingdom. I asked him what he thought the difference was between Americans and the United Kingdom when it came to the church. His statement set me back. He said, *"Bishop, Americans want to make Jesus your president and not a king."*

My thoughts were many. I replied, *"Give me some examples of kingdom."*

"Well, we serve a crown, not a country. Kingdom isn't about where you are but whom you are connected to. We are connected to the crown. We serve the king."

I remember walking with him through one of the major palaces in London, England. We walked out of the chamber where the king would stay. There were many chairs in the hallway sitting uniformly on the wall, I would say around six or seven chairs side by side. I asked, *"What are these chairs for?"*

    "They're for those who are in waiting for the king."
    "What are they waiting for?"
    "They're waiting for the King..."
    Again I asked, *"Waiting to do what?"*

    He looked at me with frustration and with sarcasm he said, *"You Americans. They're waiting to do whatever the king needs them to do."*

    I couldn't believe that all of those chairs were there just for people to wait. Why not have one person wait and let him go get the others as the king needed them?

    Bishop Ceirion said, *"You don't get it.* ***The king doesn't wait on the people... the people wait on the king!"***

    Wow, it hit me! I saw the verse in the Bible come to life: ***"But those who wait on the Lord shall renew their strength..." Isaiah 40:31 NKJV***

    The second meaning of Judah is "Yada." Yada means "to know." It has the intention of sexual intimacy in the Hebrew. The word "to know" is all over the Bible. When you see the phrase, "Adam knew Eve..." and "Abraham knew Sarah...", that word <u>knew</u> means YADA. This word is used because they were intimate and produced an offspring. "Adam knew Eve and they conceived a son named Seth..."; "Abram knew Sarah and bore a son named Isaac."

    This level of praise is more intimate. It is more God focused and not time focused. We preach the gospel because of the fallen sin of man. There would be no need for preaching if man had not sinned in the garden because we would still be praising and worshipping God. Preaching is for the past sins; praise is for our future experiences. YADA is when God and I become one.

"Not everyone who says to Me, 'Lord, Lord,' shall enter the kingdom of heaven, but he who does the will of My Father in heaven. Many will say to Me in that day, 'Lord, Lord, have we not prophesied in Your name, cast out demons in Your name, and done many wonders in Your name? And then I will declare to them, 'I never knew you; depart from Me, you who practice lawlessness!" Matthew 7: 21-23 NKJV

Jesus said in verse 23 that He never knew them. Jesus was saying, *"We never "YADA! Show me where we produced anything together."* This is eye opening. I want to become one with my Lord. I want to be so committed and so persuaded that I will praise Him until the walls fall down. I want my King, the Monarch to walk in our services and become one with us. so that we can produce, "YADA" together. See how powerful praise is!

The third word for praise is "YAD." This is where we begin to witness the supernatural and unusual just like in Acts 19:11, *"God worked unusual miracles for Paul..."* *YAD means axle, which represents "Turn Around."* An axle is the rod that fits in the center of a thing so that it has the ability to rotate. Without an axle, a wheel is useless. The axle gives the wheel is ability to spin. Without PRAISE, there is no axle in the house of God to turn things around. Jesus is the Axle. He is the Rod that comes and gets in the center of our situations, crises and problems. Jesus comes in to turn things around in our favor.

So, we first have to come together and be the Judah tribe. We must throw up our hands, shout and bring in the Monarch, Jesus! Then, we must move into a time of worship where we YADA in God's presence. We allow the Spirit of God to mingle with the spirit of man. This is where we pick up God's seed to produce God's character in us. Then we YAD, we begin to witness things in our lives turning in our favor.

God is faithful to His promises and laws. All we have to do is obey them. This is not difficult to do. All we have to do is love God more. I heard a song years ago that simply said, "Love God, Hate Sin!" That is all we have to do to turn things around.

Conclusion

I could write so much about the faithfulness of God. This book is by no means an exhaustive list or study on the **F.O.G. (Faithfulness of God)**

My intention is to strike an interest in you on the nature and character of God so that you will begin to develop a curiosity in pursuing *The Lord Jesus Christ.*

God is not mean or awful. He is not angry with us and doesn't desire to destroy us. The word of God tells us that God is slow to anger and quick to forgive. God understands the law of process better than we do. He took seven days to create what could have only taken Him a moment. God wanted to teach us the law of process.

Not everything in our lives has to be complete or perfect for it to be good. In the creation process of the world, God would look at what was done at the end of each day, and though it wasn't complete or perfect, He would say, "That is good."

It is still good! It is good because it is in the process of what it is supposed to be.

God has and always will be faithful to His words. Never allow anyone or anything to steer you from the fact that we serve an awesome and faithful God.

I hope and pray that this book was a blessing to you. It was an honor for me to write it and to share it with you.

If you ever need help in anyway and can't find anyone around who cares enough to take the time to help, look up to Heaven! There is a faithful and merciful God who is eager to help and will!

You can gain knowledge of what a wonderful daddy we have in Heaven in my third F.O.G (Fatherhood of God). book, "Daddy God".

Stay close to the flame of His presence and remember, no one is able to satisfy you like the Holy Spirit can.

There's no life like a Favored Life!

Love You!
Dr. G

STAY**CONNECTED,**
BE**BLESSED.**

From thoughtful articles to powerful newsletters, videos and more, www.fogzone.net is full of inspirations that will give you encouragement and confidence in your daily life.

AVAILABLE ON WWW.FOGZONE.NET

to Join the FAVORNATION and receive a weekly update text the word "FAVORNATION" to 22828

⌐LAUNCH
PASTORS AND LEADERSHIPS

Weekly Conference Calls from Dr. Grillo will help you grow in your relationship with the Lord and equip you to be everything God intends you to be.

Wednesday @ 12:00pm EST

Call: (712) 432-0075   **Playback: (712) 432-1085**
access CODE 138750#   **access CODE 138750#**

Dr. Jerry Grillo
STREAMING

Miss your local church service? Watch Dr. Grillo online, and see him LIVE.
Sundays @ 10:30am EST &
Wednesday @ 7:00pm EST

Dr. Jerry Grillo
VIDEO ARCHIVE

The Video Archive is a great way to watch Dr. Grillo where you want and when you want. Go to www.drjerrygrillo.com and click on "Encore."

CONNECT WITH US

Join the FAVORNATION on your favorite social network.

PUT DR. GRILLO IN YOUR POCKET

Get the inspiration and encouragement from Dr. Jerry Grillo on your iPhone, iPad or Android device! Our website will stream on each platform.

Thanks for helping us make a difference in the lives of millions around the world.

WWW.FOGZONE.NET

www.ingramcontent.com/pod-product-compliance
Lightning Source LLC
Chambersburg PA
CBHW060937040426
42445CB00011B/900